Honest Profits

Honest Profits

Your Hands On Guide to Successful Real Estate Investing

Robert Shemin

© 1995 Robert Shemin. All rights reserved.

Edited by: Isabel Anders

Cover illustration by: Brad Talbot

Design, typography, and text production: Mike Walker, Limbic Graphics.

ISBN 0-9649153-0-8

Big Boy Publishing
P.O. Box 128186
Nashville, TN 37212-8186
615-327-9390
1-800-396-4626

Table Of Contents

CHAPTER 1—How the Professionals Find Undervalued Properties 1

CHAPTER 2—Money: You May Not Have It, But You'd Better Know Where to Find It! 37

CHAPTER 3—What Everyone Ought To Know About Analyzing Properties 51

CHAPTER 4—Controlling, Holding, and Protecting Real Estate 57

CHAPTER 5—Turning Properties into Profit$ 73

CHAPTER 6—Right and Wrong Ways to Deal with Contractors 101

CHAPTER 7—How to Really Sell a Property 107

CHAPTER 8—Success 123

CHAPTER 9—Action Plan 129

Appendix 133

DISCLAIMER

THE INFORMATION CONTAINED IN ROBERT SHEMIN'S MATERIALS IS GENERAL INFORMATION.

YOU SHOULD CONSULT WITH YOUR ATTORNEY AND ACCOUNTANT BEFORE ACTING UPON ANY INFORMATION CONTAINED HEREIN.

This book is dedicated to my wife Patricia, my son Alexander, my parents, and all of my family, who have been so supportive.

Special thanks to Richard and Sharon Bell, who inspired me to do like this. Also, thank you to Sid and Craig Levinson, who also helped; and to Richard Courtney and Eggman Publishing.

Thank you to all of my teachers and friends in real estate: Tommy Towe, Hal Wilson, all investors before me who paved the way; and last, but not least, all of my tenants who never let a day be boring. Also, my gratitude to Mark Feemster and First Union Bank.

Special thanks to Susan Garabrandt.

MISSION STATEMENT

Not necessarily in this order:

To make money. You and I have to live in this world, which means the paying of bills.

- To help people. This book will help you. The type of real estate investing you will learn helps people, families, and communities.
- To have fun. Any job you do should be fun. If you are not having a good time working at your job, quit it. If this book had not been fun to write, it wouldn't have been written. If it is not fun for you to follow this advice, don't do it.

FOREWORD

Your Foundation for Financial Independence

Money makes money;
and the money
money makes,
makes more money.
Ben Franklin

History records the success
of men with objective
and a sense of direction.
Oblivion is the position of
small men overwhelmed by obstacles.
William H. Danforth

These days, it seems that everyone is on the real estate bandwagon. There seem to be more real estate infomercials than ever before portraying "a rosy future to riches." People get bitten by the bug and buy into the "I can be an instant millionaire" dream. For the unwary, real estate appears to offer an immediate way to the top of the income ladder.

Many of the real estate courses I see—and I've attended and/or reviewed almost all of them at one time or another—claim that they have the answer to everyone's financial need.

I don't agree.

Can anybody make money in real estate? Yes, with some exceptions. But most real estate courses and books fail because: 1) they promise too much; 2) they fail to reveal the risks associated with their methods (and some people have lost their shirt because they weren't aware that there was any risk); 3) they overwhelm you with poorly written books and seminars that seem more like a motivational seminar than anything else (sure, you need motivation—but you pay good money to listen to a cheerleader); and, 4) they reveal only a few ways to make money—which may not be suitable for you. This one-size-fits-all approach fails to take into account each individual's personal financial situation and financial goals.

I am honestly sickened by the amount of money people throw at useless books, seminars, and workshops. So I decided to share with you my own REAL real estate knowledge, even though I don't need the money. Because I am an attorney, I know how to spot risk and avoid it. Because I have an MBA, have been involved in high finance, and have negotiated more than 300 deals, I know how to spot a good deal when I see one. I strongly believe that I can teach anybody how to make money in real estate better than anyone else. Also, the do-gooder in me wants to help people.

In this book you will learn almost all aspects of making money in real estate. Most other books you've read or heard about concentrate only on one or two angles. In stark contrast, we'll explore an abundance of ways to make money. We will dissect each approach, and analyze the advantages and disadvantages associated with each one.

This is your entrance to a whole new profit center that can position you far ahead of your competition.

I bring to the real estate education industry what I believe to be the highest degree of truth, realism, and professionalism that to date has been rare in the field.

You'll learn from my experience and avoid the mistakes that I as well as others have made. You'll learn to avoid unnecessary risk and expense (which most other books do not cover), and you'll gain insights into the secrets and formulas that I have gathered from some of the nation's wealthiest real estate investors, top real estate brokers, and attorneys.

This book has been written with both the beginner and the professional in mind, and will show you exactly how to mirror my success.

From this point on you'll receive the education of a lifetime and be provided a solid grounding in the techniques that I've discovered. You'll be able to grow a very successful business in rather short order. You'll discover many amazing insights and strategies that you never could have known or comprehended unless you happened to be an attorney exposed to the number of deals I've done. Keep in mind, however, this is no "get rich quick" scheme. Can you get rich quick with what you'll learn from this course? It's possible, but don't forget—I made my money the old-fashioned way. By earning it.

I can promise you this:

When you've completed reading this book you'll have an almost unfair advantage over your competitors.

And that can be worth a fortune to you over the course of your lifetime.

The secrets that I'll reveal should remove almost every single roadblock—except inertia— that has ever stopped you from making a superior living.

I will give you answers to your most common concerns:
- How much money you will need to invest in property.
- The strategies to get money if you are presently cash-poor.

- Which areas of real estate are virtually guaranteed safe investments.
- How to make certain you can get your money out of a piece of property when you want to.
- What are the best real estate investments for the short, medium, and long term.
- How to protect yourself from typical real estate liabilities.

I'll also show you the most common mistakes that can kill your business right in front of your eyes, such as:

- Not having a business plan and no well-defined objectives based on your particular needs.
- Not constructing a cash-flow budget in advance that can help you predict your highs and lows and when to take action quickly.
- Ignoring the fact that you must buy a piece of property right, on the right terms, or let it go.
- Not analyzing key data that can tell you if you can sell the property for a profit.
- Not taking advantage of all the profit potential of a given real estate transaction.
- Not knowing who you are going to sell a property to before you buy it.
- Not knowing how to deal with tenants.
- Not knowing who your prospective tenants for a given property really are.
- Ignoring your properties and not inspecting them on a regular basis.
- Not responding to tenants' needs (a quick route to tenant problems).
- Not motivating your tenants to be repsonsible.
- Not networking with other real estate investors and others in the field that can help you.
- Not understanding and avoiding the risks of certain types of real estate profit-making transactions.

Granted, you may not have many of these skills right now, but I can assure you that you'll be able to avoid the above mistakes after reading this book. The reason: You'll have learned from my experience in the field and be able to replicate my successes.

REAL ESTATE AS YOUR HOBBY.

Almost everyone has some type of hobby. Some people collect stamps, collect coins, fix up cars, make quilts, restore antiques, all sorts of things. Real estate can be your hobby. Do not forget that not only can it be very profitable to get into real estate and look at houses, going to auctions and foreclosure sales on the weekends or in your spare time—it can also be a lot of fun. Just as some people buy, sell, and trade baseball cards, you can do the same with homes.

Every time you go out to look at a house or try to contact distressed sellers, treat it as a hobby. That is, have fun with it, enjoy it. Each time you look at a house or meet a distressed seller you'll learn something and come away with more information. Every house, every situation, and every seller is unique. Every buyer is different. You'll get to meet a lot of interesting people, hear a lot of interesting stories, see a lot of fascinating situation—and you can very quickly become an expert in real estate, as you could in any hobby of your choice. The only difference is that this hobby can make you a lot of money. Don't forget to have fun! Every house or home comes with a human comedy or drama. Learn about the people you meet. It is much better than TV!

Financing is the KEY.

Finding good deals is really not all that difficult. As you look for undervalued homes, think about how to get the money to buy them. One of the most important aspects of real estate is financing. However, it's also the hardest part about real estate. When you are inquiring about, or looking for distressed properties, keep in mind financing. For instance, if there is assumable and especially nonqualifying assumable financing, this can greatly add to the value of the property and can facilitate you taking over a property and making money. We will discuss this more in the chapter on analyzing property.

In sum:

1) You will learn about almost every known technique for profiting in real estate, as discussed in almost every other book, tape, and seminar available in the marketplace (and then some).

2) You will learn about the advantages and disadvantages of each profit-making method so that *you* can make an intelligent choice about which options work best for your financial situation and time considerations. Be wary of seminars, books, and tapes that only show you a couple of ways to make money and fail to point out any of the risks involved.

3) You will find an Action Plan chapter at the end of the book which contains simple, specific things you can begin to do today, this week, or this month to help get you started. Your first deal is always the hardest one. The Action Plan chapter helps you along so it's easier to be productive.

4) If you are currently active in real estate investing, this book will teach you how to substantially increase your income, provide you with new approaches to your current investments, and show you how to be more efficient.

Robert's Rule:

Whatever you do, whoever you are, you need a plan. This book will provide you with an action plan, but you must create your own plan as well. Think about it now. Write some of it down. When you finish this book, write your plan down again. Review your plan every week, or at least every month. Follow your plan, revise it, expand it—but at the very least, set yourself apart from the rest, *those who do not have a plan.*

So, read on. Learn. Do! And prosper!

MAKE A PLAN

My 1-Month Plan:
My 6-Month Plan:
My 1-Year Plan:
My 5-Year Plan:
My 20-Year Plan:
Personal Family Goals:
Spiritual Goals:
Vacation Goals:
Fun Goals:
Financial Goals—Income/Wealth-Building/Asset Goals:
Real Estate Goals:
Write down examples of each.

INTRODUCTION

You have taken the first step. By buying this book you have begun a process that can change your life. Whether you buy only one home or 200 homes, this material could make and save you thousands, tens of thousands, or millions of dollars.

Real estate has made more millionaires in America than just about any other endeavor. It is real—you can see it, touch it, live in it, and profit from it. By buying, selling, renovating, and holding residential real estate you can make a lot of money, help provide quality housing to families, and have a lot of fun.

The following materials are based upon my own experience of buying over 100 properties in the past four years, rehabilitating and managing over 150 rental units, and helping dozens of other people begin to invest in real estate.

Moreover, these materials are based upon the experiences of numerous other people who have taught me. Therefore, you are the beneficiary of all of their years of actual experience.

Learn from me—and them—and from our mistakes. This book will save you dozens of headaches and many thousands of dollars.

Here is what you will get:

1) **Every possible way that the professionals find the good deals.** If you cannot find a good deal—a property that you can buy for less than what it is worth—you cannot begin. This is probably the most important part, and what successful real estate investing turns on: How to find the deals.

2) **Financing.** Financing is fundamental to real estate investing. You will learn how to get your financial goals and game plan put into action, based on your personal objectives and particular situation. You will learn of every possible way to buy property with no money down and be schooled in the financial ins and outs of real estate. There is no better wealth builder than real estate—and I will show you why.

3) You will learn **how to analyze** real estate quickly and efficiently like the pros. You will learn how to overcome any lack of knowledge on your part about repairs, construction costs, etc. Then you will learn how to write contracts and structure your deals better than many attorneys, by reading:

4) **Controlling, promoting, and protecting real estate.** You will learn step by step how to make short-term profits quickly without using your own money. Also, you will be taught about easy methods known to **keep** your short-, medium-, and long-term wealth gained from real estate. The advantages and disadvantages of each method will be disclosed to you.

5) Next learn **how to let the government pay you rent for your rental**

properties. You will find everything you need to know . . .

6) Following that is **how to be the best landlord.** You will carefully learn how to systematize and professionalize your landholding business.

7) In Chapter Two you will be instructed step by step as to how to **sell a property.**

8) Then, as a bonus section, you will receive dozens of valuable pointers **to make you become successful.** These tables of information will exponentially increase your success ratios.

9) The next bonus is a detailed week-by-week **Action Plan** to help you really get started. In it will be simple tasks for you to do—either full time or part time—to get started. And, if you have already invested, this will help turbo-charge your real estate business.

10) Bonus #3 is The Appendix—which is full of valuable letters, documents, and analysis sheets that will help you in all facets of your business.

CHAPTER 1

How the Professionals Find Undervalued Properties

Nothing in the world can take the place of persistence.
Talent will not;
nothing is more common than unsuccessful men with talent.
Genius will not; the world is full of educated derelicts.
Persistence and determination alone are omnipotent.
The slogan 'press on' has solved and always will solve
the problems of the human race.
Calvin Coolidge

Robert's Rule:

You must always be searching for motivated sellers. Remember, if a seller is not motivated, you will not find a good deal.

Obviously, the *key* to making money and being successful in real estate is *finding* undervalued properties. If you don't find the properties you can neither turn them into instant profits nor turn them into long-term profits, such as good rental properties. Sounds simple, doesn't it?

Well, it can be if you know what you're doing.

Before you can begin making money in real estate, you must find a good deal. Here's how.

In this chapter I will provide a brief overview of how all the professionals and seminars recommend finding undervalued properties. Most of these so-called "experts" and seminars, however, fail to go into real detail about how to actually do it. They just think that by telling you to "find undervalued properties" they've done their job. Unfortunately, few things in life are that easy. It's time to put some meat on the bones!

In this chapter I will actually reveal, in detail, all the possible ways of finding undervalued properties. Then I will give you the advantages and disadvantages of each method and, at the end of the book, provide you with an Action Plan chapter. Turn to the Action Plan chapter to learn how to start finding truly undervalued properties, **today**—properties that you can turn into either short-term or long-term profits. In the following chapters, we'll tell you how to profit from finding those properties. But you cannot profit until you find the properties.

Many of the methods that I am going to reveal seem very simple. In point of fact, they are. However, these simple methods are often the most overlooked and the most effective. Oddly enough, many of the so-called experts fail to take advantage of them. On the other hand, I know non-experts (your everyday real estate investor) who make a living every year just by using *one* or *two* of the following methods.

1. LOOKING IN YOUR LOCAL NEWSPAPER.

When I'm looking in the newspaper and I find what I think is a good deal, I call immediately, because I know that if the deal really *is* that good, many people (just like you and I) are going to call. Typically, you'll find that "FSBOs" (For Sale By Owner) may be the best deal because the owner has not yet worked with a real estate agent, and usually is anxious to sell the property. Also, the seller is looking to avoid paying real estate commissions, thereby saving money for everyone.

This is not to say that a property listed with a real estate agent cannot be a good deal through careful negotiation. Many people, however, believe that once a real estate agent has gotten hold of a property, it is going to be sold for retail, not for wholesale; and you very much want to be a *wholesale buyer*. Though real estate agents serve an important role, sometimes they may tell the sellers that they can get them a very high *retail* value for the property, just so they'll get the listing. Very often the actual sales price is way below the price quoted by the realtor. That is how realtors sell properties and make commissions.

Newspapers also serve as a cheap and easy way to educate yourself about the market in which you will be investing. If you continually look at the newspaper every week, you will quickly learn what markets, house types, and prices make the most sense for you. The newspaper lists properties by certain areas, certain features, and also sometimes by price. By analyzing newspaper ads and actually getting in your car and looking at some of the real estate, you'll quickly discover what "retail value" means, what "good values" are, and where to find the "bargains."

How the Professionals Find Undervalued Properties

Saturday and Sunday editions of the newspaper are the best. Look throughout the whole section, but specifically for properties listed under *"Investments,"* under areas in which you plan to concentrate, and particularly noting *"For Sale By Owners" ("FSBOs")*. Believe it or not, *many of my best deals have been found right in the newspaper.*

Remember, local papers, neighborhood weeklies, and any newspaper that has real estate ads can be a great source.

Another important reason to read the real estate section in your newspaper every day (or at least every weekend) is to learn about real estate auctions (discussed below).

Again, even though it sounds so simple and so obvious, you could probably make a living just from the newspaper, as many people do.

Advantages: **Easy to do. No real cost to you.**

Disadvantages: **Everyone has access to the newspaper, so competition is fierce.**

Robert's Rule:

Every time you look at a house you learn something.

---

2. DRIVING FOR DOLLARS (SEARCHING NEIGHBORHOODS).

Another seemingly simple and obvious way to locate homes that you can buy way under the market is driving the neighborhoods and looking around. Although this seems blatantly obvious, this is a tactic that many of these high-priced seminars and real estate experts teach. And it works! I personally know people who make a living from real estate just by driving certain neighborhoods that they concentrate on, finding addresses on mailboxes, talking to neighbors and strangers, looking for vacant homes and people who need to sell their homes in a hurry for under market prices.

When you drive around a neighborhood that you think may be of interest to you, look for the following real estate signs: "For Sale," "For Sale By Owner" ("FSBO") and "For Rent," and copy down the telephone numbers if you spot a house that interests you. **FSBO** means that a property is for sale without the aid of a real estate agent. Therefore, you can negotiate directly with the seller who may be in a hurry to sell the property.

"**For Rent**" properties most likely means that the property is owned by a real estate investor and/or managed by a property management company. If the unit is empty and is not generating any income, the owner may be motivated to sell the property. Either contact the owner or the property management company (if there is one) directly, and let it be known that you are interested in purchasing the property. *The property management company may also be a good source* for finding other owners who are motivated to sell their properties.

Regular real estate company "For Sale" signs are also worth following up on for two reasons. First, you may actually find a good deal. Second, it will give you a good idea of what *retail* value is when you compare other homes in the neighborhood.

Robert's Rule

A small, "crummy," or difficult to spot "For Sale" or "For Rent" sign means a better deal for you. Why? Since the sellers are not marketing their property effectively, you may be the only one who realizes that the property is even for sale. Have you heard of a "Buyers' Market"? In many of these cases, you may be the only "market"—a market of one.

Look for **abandoned properties**, vacant homes, homes that look like they are in need of serious repair (e. g., boarded-up homes), and homes where the yards have not been cut or have a lot of trash around them. Also, look for homes that have "**Condemned**" or "Uninhabitable" signs. Condemned properties can be gold mines. In almost every case, the owner of such a property either has to (or would very much like to) get rid of such a home. Houses may be condemned for many reasons, including health and safety factors (they may have had fires, their plumbing or electrical systems may not be safe, etc.) Many condemned homes need a lot of work, while some do not need much work at all. They may just be "unfit for human habitation" due to a simple plumbing, electrical, or roof problem which could be inexpensive to fix. If a house is condemned, contact your local Code Administrator (at the local City Housing Offices), who will be glad to provide you with a list of code violations and/or reasons why the house has been condemned.

Many serious real estate pros are what we call "**rehabilitators**" of homes; that is, people who buy properties in bad shape, fix them up, and sell them at a profit.

How the Professionals Find Undervalued Properties

Many "rehabbers" deal only in "condemned" properties and make a great living.

Get the addresses of any and all vacant properties, and those that need major repairs. Talk to the neighbors and find out who owns the property. If that fails, you can also access this information with a phone call or a visit to the tax assessor's office, where the ownership of all homes is on public record. Find out who the owners are and how you can contact them. Follow up with a phone call or letter to the owners, indicating that you may be interested in buying their property.

One of the most successful tactics that I have used is *talking to neighbors*. It sounds so simple, but it works! Neighbors are a wealth of information. If you are surveying a neighborhood on a Saturday or Sunday, or in the evening, you may find many of the neighbors out. Most likely, they will be able to tell you who the owners are, where they are, why the property is abandoned or in disrepair (perhaps there was a death or a divorce in the family; or maybe they've run into financial troubles and need to sell the property). The neighbors may also be able to tell you about other properties that may be available or fit the criteria you are looking for.

Again, just like looking in newspapers, driving through neighborhoods will educate you in an inexpensive and easy manner. You'll learn what the neighbors and neighborhood is like, get an idea of prices and rents in that area (by calling on all For Sale, For Rent, and FSBO homes), and perhaps, most importantly, get an idea of which neighborhoods are "in transition." "In transition" neighborhoods are those where homes are being fixed up and property values seem to be on the rise. If you can find a deal in one of those neighborhoods, don't hesitate to buy it. You may also find neighborhoods that are not in transition, that are sinking down, that seem to be in disrepair and getting worse. Stay away!

You can make a living by driving through neighborhoods. When you find an address that may be of interest to you, copy down the address. You can call the property tax assessor's office and get the owners' name and address. It is of public record. If you have a lot of addresses you may want to:

1. Look them up at the Registrar of Deeds' office. The employees there should be helpful.

2. Have a real estate agent or a computer whiz with access to the property tax roll computer data base look up the owners for you. Almost all real estate agents can access this and might be glad to help you in hopes that they can make you a client.

Make a habit of looking for houses whenever you are driving.

Fact: Recently, I spent a total of an hour and a half driving certain areas and found six potentially great deals that I eventually made thousands of dollars of profit on.

Fact: I know of a young man who spends all day every Saturday driving up and down streets, copying down the addresses of vacant homes and phone numbers listed on "For Sale" signs. He finds the great deals, puts them under contract, and sells them to other investors for some big dollars. He makes thousands of dollars per house and never seems to be lacking for inventory—simply by driving through the neighborhoods!

Advantages: **You will find many good deals. There is simply no better way to learn about a neighborhood.**

Disadvantages: **This method takes time and patience. Be careful when getting out and looking at homes. If you are in a tough neighborhood, take someone with you.**

Robert's Rule: Safety

Unfortunately, safety has to be a concern for everyone today. If you become a real estate investor, you will very often be going into transitional neighborhoods. Always err on the side of caution.

Here are some pointers:

- **Never go into a dangerous area or get out of your car if you do not feel safe.**
- **If you have to go into a vacant house, always knock loudly and speak loudly to determine if anyone is around.**
- **Wait a few minutes before entering to allow any persons there to make their presence known.**
- **Don't go into vacant property alone, unless you're sure nobody is in there.**
- **Always be aware of who is around you. If someone is nearby who makes you uncomfortable, leave immediately.**
- **Do not drive expensive or flashy cars into transitional or low-income neighborhoods.**

3. FORECLOSURES.

Foreclosures are an excellent example of finding truly undervalued properties. The name itself connotes a bargain. What does foreclosure mean? A foreclosure occurs when property owners have not paid their mortgage and the lending institution (a

How the Professionals Find Undervalued Properties

bank, the Federal Housing Authority—FHA, the Veterans' Administration—VA, etc.) has taken (or is in the process of taking) the property back due to nonpayment.

The most common sources for finding foreclosed property are HUD (Housing and Urban Development), the VA, banks, finance companies, lawyers, and the Notice of Foreclosures which can be found in the local legal newspaper (and sometimes your local paper). Most likely, the HUD list can be found in your local Sunday newspaper. And many times the VA list of foreclosures is also in your newspaper. Contact your local HUD and/or VA office and get a list of properties for sale if you cannot find it in the local papers, or contact a real estate agent in order to get the lists.

The VA guarantees loans for veterans so that they can buy homes. Unfortunately, many of these veterans do not make their mortgage payments and the VA has to take their home back. The HUD and/or FHA help first-time home buyers buy a home by guaranteeing the loans. They guarantee a tremendous number of loans all around the country every day. Many first-time home buyers get in over their head, or come into financial trouble and cannot make their mortgage payments. Sometimes, HUD and the VA reclaim these homes and offer them for sale.

Sometimes these federal organizations offer such properties at below market prices. If anything, you will have to shop hard and search very intensely to find bargains; but they do exist. For the first year and a half that I was in real estate, I bought almost exclusively from the HUD list. HUD was offering very attractive financing on duplexes if I put 15% down. These financing packages are available around the country, though they may differ a little by region. Always keep in mind that HUD and the VA are constantly taking back homes and offering them at attractive prices with attractive financing almost everywhere.

Like HUD and the VA, banks, credit companies, "corner of the shopping mall" loan companies, and second mortgage companies have to take back real estate. When one of these institutions repossesses a property, it is known as a bank repossession (**"Repo"**). Most banks and lending institutions do not want to be in the real estate business and are very anxious to have this real estate sold and get it "off the books."

You will need to call these banks and ask for the Real Estate Owned (**"REO"**) **Department** or the **Special Asset Department.** The bank will often provide a list of repossessed properties and their corresponding prices. Many times a savvy real estate investor can negotiate with the bank because, in actuality, the bank just wants to recapture the amount of money it loaned on the property. Usually, the bank is not interested in making a profit; it is just hoping to get rid of the real estate. In other words, even if a bank has a mortgage of $50,000 on a house and the house has a market value of $80,000, the bank will often forego trying to make a profit so long as it can recover the initial loan ($50,000 plus costs). There is a possibility that one can negotiate with the bank and buy that house for $20,000–30,000 below the market value of the property. Of course, finding these types of deals depends on your local economy and the state of health of the lending institutions. At certain times, and in certain areas, banks take a lot of properties back and look to sell them as quickly as possible. On the other hand, in some areas around the country, banks are not taking many properties back and are not as anxious to sell them. Nevertheless, there are always properties being foreclosed.

Depending on your state and location, if owners have not paid their mortgage, the lending institution (federal or private) will foreclose on their property. In order to

---

Robert's Rule:

Regardless of the state of the economy, it is very important to develop good relationships with your local banks and lending institutions (including many of the second mortgage companies). By improving your relationship with the banks, you may find that you'll be the first person they call when they want to get rid of a property quickly. This is an excellent way of finding undervalued properties, and many times the lending institutions will offer favorable financing on the property, just to get the property sold and/or "off the books."

---

do that, the institution must make public a notice that it is going to foreclose on this property. Many cities, municipalities, counties, and various areas of the country have a legal newspaper in which these public notices appear. You can ask almost any knowledgeable attorney or bank officer where foreclosures are publicized, and review this publication and/or receive it monthly.

Many times these notices are taken out in a very legalized form which may at first glance appear difficult to read. However, I must emphasize this list as an incredible source of finding real estate that you can buy way below market.

I personally know people who make an entire living just through reviewing the public notice of foreclosures. In fact, many seminars and real estate experts concentrate solely on this one area as a source of finding undervalued properties. Later we will explain, with examples, how to read, understand, and profit from these foreclosure notices. It is imperative that you find out where foreclosures are publicized in your area and get those lists, learn how to read the lists, and (as I will show you later) learn how to profit from them.

How the Professionals Find Undervalued Properties

Probably one of the best sources of undervalued properties can be found in the foreclosures of the second-tier lending institutions. These institutions typically offer loans to people who have been turned down by the banks. You've probably seen a few of them advertised on television or in strip shopping centers: The Money Store, Associates Financial, and other types of quick home loan places.

These types of institutions loan money to higher risk borrowers at higher interest rates. Usually, they will have a few foreclosures. Find these institutions (look in your Yellow Pages). Start a friendship with them. Let them know what you do. Get them to call you or send you a list of new foreclosures on a continuing basis. You may even find that many of these institutions will offer you financing as well.

WHY ARE THERE FORECLOSURES?

WHY DO PEOPLE LET THEIR HOUSES GO FOR BELOW MARKET PRICES?

Probably the #1 reason why homes are foreclosed upon is *divorce*. Many families today depend on two incomes to support the family and make the house payments. Divorce usually results in only one of the income earners staying in the home, and normally that person cannot afford it. Therefore, divorce is often the cause of foreclosure.

Also, unfortunately, *unemployment* is a leading cause of foreclosures. Many times the *death* of the breadwinner will lead to the house going into foreclosure. Another cause is *balloon payments* on a mortgage; that is, there is a loan for 10-20 years in which the balance is due in perhaps 3-10 years. Many times when the people obtained the loan they anticipated that their income would go up, and they would be able to pay off the entire balance. The balloon payment becomes due and the owner cannot make the payment. Then the mortgage holder, who is oftentimes the seller, has to foreclose on the property because the mortgagor, the person to whom the loan was made, is unable to come up with all the money for the balloon payment.

Sometimes people move out of town, or are transferred in their job, and just let the house go. Sometimes people move to start over, to get a fresh start. If they have too much debt, they walk away from their house and let it be foreclosed upon. Distress sales may not be foreclosures, but the sales must be done very quickly for many different reasons. Again, often divorce, unemployment, balloon payments, or a death in the family are causes of distress sales. This is when the seller has to sell very quickly and must get as much cash as possible.

Oftentimes foreclosure is imminent; that is, the owners are behind on their payment, or soon going to be behind on their payments. Often they have too much debt and they must get rid of the house quickly and raise as much cash as possible. Attorneys, accountants, and real estate agents are good sources for finding these distress sales, as are newspaper ads and all of the other methods we discussed. When one partner dies, oftentimes the house is left to the estate or to the children or relatives. Sometimes a widow no longer wants to live in the house, and/or cannot afford to make the payments. Also, with estate sales, many times the children are scattered all over the country or the world and have no interest in the house. Then they just want to get as much money as they can out of it, quickly and easily. These are what we call distress sales, which spell opportunities for you.

Many times unexpected bills or expenses can lead to foreclosure. For instance, medical problems that people have to pay for out of their own pocket, and expensive, ongoing medical procedures can often lead to a drastic change in the property owners' financial position, and unfortunately to foreclosure and/or distress sales.

A Quick Lesson in Foreclosures.

Many people are familiar with a first mortgage, second mortgage, first deed of trust, and second deed of trust. And most people are familiar with foreclosure. But few people understand how a foreclosure sale actually works. All the world seems to have a pecking order. This is the case with foreclosure sales.

If you hold a first mortgage—that is, you loaned the money to someone and took out a first mortgage against a property—you are first in line. If you are the second person in line and in time to loan money, you would be the second mortgagee. There can be a third, fourth, fifth, six, etc., mortgage also. Suppose you have a first mortgage on the property, and the person to whom you lent money does not pay you back, and you want to foreclose. If there is only enough equity in the property to pay you, everyone behind you would be wiped out.

At a foreclosure sale, if I am the first mortgage holder and people bid more than the present value of my mortgage, then I get all of the money owed to me. Whatever money is left over goes to the second mortgage holder; and if there is still money left, then it goes to the third, fourth, fifth, and sixth, on down the line.

Public Records Can Be Your Gold Mine.

All notices of foreclosure must be recorded down at your local courthouse. It would be most beneficial to you to learn how your public recordation system works regarding real estate. I am sure that if you ask nicely, the people at your local recordation office will explain how things work. It is not really that difficult, it just

How the Professionals Find Undervalued Properties

takes a little time to understand the system. One could easily spend a few hours, a few days, or a lifetime at the courthouse looking for newly recorded documents regarding foreclosures.

There is an individual in my town who is one of the most successful real estate wheeler dealers because he has befriended most of the people in the courthouse and the Registrar of Deeds (where the real documents are recorded). They are happy to direct him to newly recorded documents concerning foreclosures. He spends quite a bit of time (he even brings the employees popcorn when he is there) almost every day at the courthouse, and he gets more leads than he ever needs concerning foreclosures and distress sales of real estate.

Perhaps you may not want to spend your lifetime looking up documents at your local courthouse. But it would be very beneficial for you to spend at least a day or two down there, learning how the system works, learning how to look up properties, and gathering information concerning properties. You also can look at documents that have just been recorded and see if any notices of foreclosure have been recorded; then contact those institutions. At first, all of these records may seem overwhelming; but with a little persistence and a lot of questions you soon will be able to understand this system as well as any attorney.

These systems may vary slightly from county to county, but they are all basically the same. By going down there and reviewing documents, you'll soon learn how to look up and understand mortgages, judgments, taxes, abstracts of title, liens, IRS and state tax liens, lis pendens, trust deeds, and all other types of liens and real estate documents. Some states are, or soon will be, "on line" with deed and title information. Use your computer or ask a friend who is computer literate to do title searches for good deals.

A Brief Description of How to Use Public Records to Research a Real Estate Title, Real Estate Complaints, Defaults, Judgments, and Lawsuits.

As you are interested in distressed properties, you are constantly searching for foreclosures or property that will soon be in foreclosure. Depending on which state you live in, this information can be obtained through the following: Sheriff's notice of sales, Commissioner's notice of sales, or a simple review of the court docket—that is, if the court obtains the real estate foreclosures' judgments. Be on the lookout for Sheriff's sales, notice of equity sales, foreclosure, or foreclosure notices. In trustee states, be on the lookout for notices of trustees' sales, notice of defaults.

Each locality may call these things by different names, but your local courthouse officials, Registrar of Deeds, or friendly attorney can easily explain all of this to you. Find out from your local courthouse where notices of foreclosures are filed, which courts handle cases concerning foreclosures and proceedings against homeowners or mortgagors (the people who borrowed money and are in debt). As stated earlier, most states require publication of the notice of default—and you can easily find out in which publication these appear by contacting a friendly attorney.

Most Registrars of Deeds or public offices where real estate records are recorded have what is called a general index. This general index may be on microfiche cards, microphone cassette, or maybe on computerized printouts. Once you find a name of a person who is in default or who is a mortgagor or owner of a property, look up that name in the general index. Almost all documents pertaining to that person or that property are filed there. This may sound complicated; but more than likely there are people who work at these offices who are paid to help answer your questions. They'll be more than happy to explain the system to you. Many localities use a filing system called the book and page system. Or they may have a reel and image system, which is used in major metropolitan areas. Less populated counties normally use book and page.

The book and page system. The book and page system is as it sounds. All the property information you will be looking for will be recorded in a particular book, on a particular page which you can find in the general index. Once you find what you are looking for by name, it will refer you to book and page. Then you go to the actual book and the correct page and find the information you need. Sometimes, especially in larger cities, this information is not in an actual book, but has been recorded on microfiche or in a computer system. Viewers are provided for the public in the offices where these documents are recorded.

Once you learn the ins and outs of the system, you can look at many properties very rapidly. The document numbers and the date should be easy to locate, once you find the information you need.

Before you buy any property, either you or your attorney should research every deed, trust, or lien recorded against that property. Each deed of trust or mortgage will reference the amount and the interest rate, and who the mortgagor is. These are called liens against the property. Before you buy a foreclosed property, or before you buy from a distressed seller, you should know of all the liens concerning the property.

In the beginning it would probably be best for you to hire an attorney to show you how he/she checks the title. It would be very beneficial for you to learn how to do it, so you could then go down to the courthouse and look at these documents yourself. However, until you are very familiar and very thorough concerning searching for these documents, you would probably be better off spending your valuable time looking for these distressed sellers and hiring an attorney and/or title company to do these title searches for you.

What is a LIS PENDENS?

If in your title searches you find a "lis pendens" or a property that has a lis pendens filed against it, it is a lis that is pending. It simply means that this is a notice that there is some type of judgment pending against the property. It can be almost any type of legal action that has been filed against the property; for instance, an action to obtain money from the property owner for something related or unrelated to the property. It is a lien against the property. If it is filed after the foreclosing trust deed or mortgage, and that trust deed or mortgage is in foreclosure, then it will be extinguished.

If it is a lis pendens that has been filed before a foreclosing mortgage, then it will not be extinguished at the foreclosure sale. Again, where does that lis pendens appear on the pecking order? If it is below the mortgage that is foreclosing, it will be extinguished; if it is above the mortgage that is being foreclosed then it will remain with the property.

Quit Claim Deeds.

Quit Claim Deeds are exactly what they sound like. I quit my claim. Most states recognize the legality and power of a quit claim deed. Some states such as California have restrictions on them. Please check your state for the value of the quit claim. I can quit claim my property to you. That means whatever interest I have or whatever claim I have on the property, I quit it to you. Therefore, whatever I had, you have. However, because a quit claim is limited in its power; that is, I quit whatever I have to you—you take whatever claim that may be from this property (it may be a good one or a bad one). Most title companies require or prefer, in order to insure good title, a grant deed or a warranty deed. These deeds are also exactly as they sound. A warranty deed means that I warrant this deed to you. Just as your refrigerator comes with a warranty and guarantees, so does this warranty deed. It is a stronger and more powerful form of conveyance or transferring of property, because it warranties and/or guarantees the deed to you.

Title Insurance.

Title insurance is exactly what it sounds like, too. It insures title. Title insurance companies, such as Chicago Title or Stewart Title, are insurance companies that insure property title. It is highly recommended that you get title insurance whenever you buy property.

Honest Profits

Many times it is customary for the sellers to pay for this insurance. That is, they are insuring that the title they give you is good. The title company will do their own, or have their own lawyers do a title search and give you a title insurance policy. At every closing you go to, make sure you read and understand this title insurance policy, as it may have exceptions in the back. Most of the time these exceptions are what is called utility easements; that is, easements allowing utility companies to run lines or water pipes or sewers across your property. These should really be no problem for you, as you wouldn't mind having these utilities available to your house. However, make sure you understand all the exceptions on your title policy.

For some reason down the road, or perhaps when you sell this property with title insurance on it, if there is a problem with the title, *the title company has insured the title* and will defend you in any actions concerning this title. Therefore, just as with most types of insurance, if you have title insurance you don't have to worry about the quality of your title, as long as you understand any exceptions in that policy. When you become aware of distress properties and are not sure about their title, the way to make yourself sure is to have a title company or an attorney do a search of the property and provide all the documentation and explanations to you. This may cost some money; for instance, it usually costs me $100–150. But many times it is worth it, especially when you are starting out—to fully understand how real estate titles and liens work.

Robert's Rule:

Never buy property without title insurance. You always want to know that there is a clear title to the property that you are buying.

Other Liens.

Other types of liens that may be on the property are tax liens. These can be filed by federal taxing authorities (IRS), state or local taxing authorities. Please contact your local tax offices and/or Registrar of Deed offices to find out what order these liens take on a property and/or foreclosure sale. A good local attorney will also be able to instruct you on these matters. Most localities have tax sales; that is, if a property owner did not pay the property taxes on a piece of property for a certain amount of time, the city, state, or local taxing authority may or may not advertise these tax sales and auction these properties off. These can be very lucrative, but you must check on the right of redemption; that is, how long the original owner has the right to redeem, or pay those taxes, and get the property back.

Many times, even if you buy a property at a tax sale, and, sometime later, according to the local law, the original property owner comes and pays those taxes and takes the property back, you will be granted a rate of interest for the money you had invested in the property. That rate of interest may vary from state to state and can oftentimes be very high. Thus, local tax sales can be very profitable. Either you can end up owning the property for little money, if the previous owner does not redeem it; or you can make a good return on your money.

Federal tax liens are unique unto themselves. There is a 120-day waiting period for the federal government to exercise its right of redemption. That is, if there is a federal (IRS) tax lien on a property, the federal government has 120 days to come in and protect its lien, or it has a 120-day right of redemption. So if there is a federal tax lien on a property, that can cloud the title for 120 days.

Most title insurance companies will not insure title on a property for 120 days if there is a federal tax lien, because during that 120 days the IRS can come in and take over that property. If a federal tax lien is found, the party handling the sale—or perhaps you, who are interested in purchasing the property—can ask if the federal government has been notified of the approaching sale or foreclosure. The law requires that the government be given a 25-day notice of the sale. If the government is not notified, the lien will not be extinguished with the expiration of the 120-day right of redemption.

Mechanics Liens.

Many localities, cities, and states, allow people who work on houses—that is contractors, painters, plumbers—to file what are called mechanics man's liens. That is, they did the work on a house but were not paid, and they filed their own lien on a house. The local rules regarding these liens vary from locality to locality, and you should be made familiar with them.

A mechanics lien can sometimes take precedent over all other liens and can easily cloud a title. Therefore, you must make sure that there are no mechanics liens filed on a property before you become interested in it.

Though much of this may sound confusing, a local attorney or someone in your Registrar of Deeds' office or local office where documents regarding real estate are recorded can explain these liens, rules, and regulations to you very easily. It is most important that you understand all this; so I would recommend that you spend some time with a local attorney or some time in your local recording office to find out, research, ask a lot of questions, and understand all of the above liens and government

Honest Profits

rules and regulations. Information is power; and if you have a lot of the above information and understand it, you will possess a tremendous amount of power and will be able to profit handsomely in real estate.

Foreclosures.

Advantages: **Opportunities for great deals. You can also get some good financing from the foreclosing institution such as the bank, HUD, and the VA.**

Disadvantages: **Be careful. Just because something is in foreclosure does not mean it is a good deal. Why was it foreclosed upon? Beware of title problems. Get title insurance.**

4. AUCTIONS.

Auctions are another source of finding below-market-priced houses and other real estate. I personally have found some really good deals at auctions; but, to be honest, they are few and far between.

Although it is not easy to find "bargains" at auctions, I have learned a great deal from being in attendance. The price at which a house sells at auction is typically a true indication of market value. Why? The auction is publicized for many weeks before the auction, usually with yard signs and in your local paper. At the time of auction, anyone interested in purchasing that type of property will show up (sometimes people who aren't interested in the property show up and watch as people bid on the house). It is usually very exciting; whoever bids the highest wins at the auction.

Auctions are gaining in popularity. Selling a home quickly and easily is the main reason for having an auction. Quite often, a seller does not want to list the house with a real estate agent or go the FSBO (For Sale By Owner) route. Sometimes that might mean waiting months until the "right" buyer comes along—even if the seller thinks that an agent can get a higher price. In fact, because auctions are gaining in popularity, many homes are now selling close to (or even above) full value at auctions.

An auction represents the highest form of capitalism. By attending auctions, you will get a first-class education in real estate. First, you will see demand, supply, and various market forces in action. Second, and most importantly, you will meet many other people who are interested in or are buying investment real estate; in other words, you will be forming your "**Network**."

Every time I go to an auction, I work the crowd as though it is the most important cocktail party of my life. I try to meet everyone there, get all their names, phone numbers, and what they do. Down the road you will find these people will become your clients when *you* find undervalued properties. By creating this network, you will

How the Professionals Find Undervalued Properties

have built yourself a database of many people who buy and sell properties for investment purposes. Later, when you find an undervalued property, you'll be able to call your network and *"flip"* or sell the house to one of them. They can also become sources of good deals for you.

Most auctions are highly publicized in the newspapers; some, however, are not. Call local auction companies and get on their mailing lists. They will send you

---

Robert's Rule: Secrets of Bidding at an Auction

1. Review the property and set *your* highest bid *before* the bidding begins. Never get caught up in the emotion of the auction and never bid above your highest bid.

2. Inspect the house and the information very carefully. Ask the following questions—the answers will help you in your bidding:

(a) Will title insurance be provided?
(b) How long do you have to close the purchase?
(c) Is the purchase cash or terms?
(d) Are there any public notices of problems, i. e., code letters? Can you test the appliances, heating, and air?
(e) How much earnest money do you have to put down?
(f) What repairs are needed and how much will they cost?

3. Never bid until the final count is given. Why? Because only the last bidder wins at an auction. The truly serious bidders come out at the end. Usually there is a three count, "going once, going twice, going three times, sold!" I always bid after the "going twice.

4. Test your opponents' patience. If you get into a bidding contest, raise your bid by only $50—100 to annoy your opponent. This takes the excitement and emotion out of the bidding and the other bidder may give up.

5. Always ask the auctioneers about other auctions and other property. They are excellent sources of good deals and sometimes they will sell them to you before an auction has been publicized.

6. Never, never get caught up in the emotions of the auction and don't bid above your pre-set limit. Remember, real estate is a business. Let logic, not emotion, rule your decisions.

---

notification of each and every auction. You can locate auction companies in the yellow pages under "auctioneers and/or real estate." Also, when you go to auctions, make sure that you give the auctioneers your name and number so they can send you information.

Honest Profits

Auctions can be very educational, very profitable, and a whole lot of fun. In the end, the most valuable information you'll get from an auction is a list of the people who buy and sell properties.

Auctions.

Advantages: **Auctions are quick, fun and very educational. You will learn market values from the auction price. More importantly, you will meet other real estate people from whom you can buy and sell. If you go to enough of them, you may eventually get an incredible deal.**

Disadvantages: **With all of the excitement at auctions, many properties sell for right at or above true value. Do not get emotional at auctions. Stay calm and directed.**

5. TAX SALES.

The Internal Revenue Service, state, and local taxing authorities all have the power and the ability to slap a powerful tax lien on a property when the owners don't pay their taxes (although it varies state to state). If the tax lien is not removed (by paying the relevant taxing authority), these agencies seize the property and sell it at a tax sale.

Each area of the country does a tax sale a little differently, but basically they are like auctions given by some of the most powerful auctioneers in the country: the IRS or the local and state taxing authority. The process begins when an individual does not pay taxes, allowing a taxing authority to place a tax lien on the property. This tax lien takes precedence over all other liens, mortgages, and debt. After a certain period of time (it varies by state), the taxing authorities will auction off property to collect on the tax lien. Most of the time these tax auctions are publicized in the local newspaper. You can also find out about them by calling the IRS and/or the state and local taxing authorities. Many areas hold their tax sales at the same time each year.

Many real estate seminars speak almost exclusively about tax sales and the great deals you can find. They can be a great deal, but one must be very careful when purchasing at a tax auction. Many states and localities have what are called "**rights of redemption.**" That is, the person who is being foreclosed upon has the right to redeem the property for a certain amount of time (it varies from state to state) after you purchase the property at a tax auction. In many states, it is one year; in some states it can be two or more years. That is, you may be buying a piece of property at a tax auction; but within a certain period of time, the buyer can return and take the property back from you. Of course, if that happens, you will receive interest on the money that you spent at the tax auction; but you can lose title to the property.

It is also difficult, but not impossible, to get title insurance on property bought at tax sales. Also, if you plan to buy houses at tax auctions, make sure you check with your local attorney and/or title/escrow companies to see how and when you can get clear title and title insurance. Again, this can be a very good way to find and purchase undervalued properties, but you must be very careful and learn the rules of your local tax sales.

Tax Sales

Advantages: **There are not a lot of people who actually bid at tax sales. A good return on your money can be realized,** *even if* **the original owners redeem their property. Sometimes, however, you can literally steal a property.**

Disadvantages: **It is almost impossible to get title insurance on a property purchased at a tax sale. Thus, you need to insure that you get an excellent title search. Also, even if you do buy the property at a tax sale, you may have to give up the property if the original owner seeks a "right ofredemption." It will take years to get clear title and/or title insurance.**

6. "BIRD DOGS."

Many real estate professionals have a network of people who find undervalued properties for them. These people are referred to affectionately as "bird dogs." That is, they sniff out and point toward a property that may turn out to be a very good deal. I often use bird dogs. I offer $500 cash if I close (that is, if I purchase) a property that someone has found for me. That person can be a friend, a repairman, a policeman, a postman who knows a certain neighborhood, a fireman who works in a certain area, or anyone who possibly can say, "Hey, here's a house, an address and/or the name of an owner who may want to sell this property at a greatly reduced price," or "I saw a boarded-up house at 20 Main Street." Friends, acquaintances, and professional contacts will prove to be excellent bird dogs.

Let everyone know that you are in the business of buying real estate and it will be amazing how many people will help you. *They will be especially helpful if you pay them.* That is, if someone brings you an address, the name of an owner; or someone who needs to sell a property at a reduced price, and you buy that property (and later turn it into profits for yourself), *pay the person a finder's fee.* This will insure that your "bird dog" will continue to look for properties and good deals *for you.* Many real estate professionals sit back and let their network of bird dogs bring potentially good deals to them. Mortgage company employees, attorneys, accountants, real estate agents, other real estate investors, government employees, public works employees, maintenance people, property managers, and landscapers all make excellent bird dogs.

> ## *Robert's Rule: How to Use a Bird Dog*
>
> Have your bird dogs bring you names, phone numbers, addresses of boarded-up homes, notices of estate sales, names of anybody getting divorced, or anyone else who needs to sell a home quickly. If all you get is an address, great! Just call the tax assessor's office to find out the owner.

Bird Dogs

Advantages: Using bird dogs frees up your personal time because you are having others do your legwork and find you great deals.

Disadvantages: It costs money. You must pay your bird dogs so they keep calling *you* and not someone else.

7. ADVERTISING.

You can find many undervalued properties by advertising yourself as one who buys properties. Look in your newspaper today and find ads that say "Cash for your house," or "Need to sell your home, please call this number." You can run these ads (and the ones we'll show you below, which I think are the best), and people who need to sell their home quickly will call you.

Here's a funny, true, and valuable story. A friend of mine once bought an abandoned building (along a busy highway) very cheaply for the sole purpose of painting "I Buy Real Estate" and his phone number on the side facing the highway. This one building was his sole form of advertising, and it has *successfully* served him for over 12 years in finding undervalued properties. This property continues to serve as a free billboard which is viewed by over 10,000 people every day.

Run "workhorse" newspaper ads.

Here are several extremely effective ads, written by one of the top copywriters in the nation. Try them and you'll see why they were well worth the top fees he charges.

(Notice that in all ads, direct mail, and the like, the idea is to use a "rifle" approach

How the Professionals Find Undervalued Properties

to target prospects. You want to pinpoint your marketing to the precise person you aim to reach.) Here are a few examples:

DO YOU NEED A MONEY MIRACLE RIGHT NOW? If you have a house in any condition that you want to sell, I've got cash, know-how, and banking connections. And I'm eager to buy your home. Please call Robert Shemin at 000-0000 right now for an extraordinary no-risk proposition.

ARE YOU STARVED FOR CASH? Do you have a house you want to sell? I've got cash, know-how, and banking connections and I'm itching to buy your home. I urge you to call Robert Shemin at 000-0000 right now for an extraordinary no-risk proposition.

ARE YOU BEHIND IN YOUR HOUSE PAYMENTS? Do you want to sell your house? I've got cash, know-how, and banking connections and I'm itching to buy your home. I urge you to call Robert Shemin at 000-0000 right now for an extraordinary no-risk proposition.

> WARNING!!
> SELL NO HOME UNTIL YOU READ THIS:
>
> Do you want to sell your house? I've got cash, know-how, and banking connections and I'm itching to buy your home. I urge you to call Robert Shemin at 000-000 right now for an extraordinary no-risk proposition.
>
> Top Real Estate Owner Looking for 6 Homes to Pay Cash for This Week! Have you got a home you want to sell? I've got cash and know-how and banking connections and I'm itching to buy your home. I urge you to call Robert Shemin at 000-000 right now for an extraordinary no-risk proposition.

Another source of advertising is direct mail. Many real estate professionals will get lists of names from the county courthouse or the phone book or other marketing sources and send out multitudes of letters introducing themselves and letting the world know that they buy houses for cash. Letters can be very effective in letting people know what business you're in and bringing many potentially good properties to you. You should also send letters to out-of-state owners and owners of boarded-up or condemned homes. Typically, these are very motivated sellers.

Direct Mail Dos and Don'ts:

- Never send a letter out bulk mail (it looks too much like junk mail and may get thrown out before it's read).
- Use a First Class Commemorative Stamp on your letter (to increase the odds the recipient opens the envelope).
- Never use an adhesive address label on the envelope.
- Never place any sort of teaser copy on the envelope. It is a good idea to write "Urgent" in red on the outer envelope.
- Place your address only in the upper left hand corner of the envelope.
- Make sure the recipient's name and address and your return address are in the same type face and look as if they were typed by the same typewriter (in order to make the correspondence appear as personal as possible, so people won't throw out your mail). A laser printer can do an excellent job.
- Only do small test mailings. Always, always, test a mailing list first by sending out no more than 1,000 letters at any one time.

- Your own compiled list will generally out-pull a "cold" mailing list you rent by a factor of 25:1.
- Let people in on the reason why you are making them an offer and you'll increase your response appreciably.
- Ask for a specific action, e. g., "Please call me at 000-0000 before such-and-such a date."
- If you have done your homework, you'll make the right offer to the right list and you'll get your letter opened and acted upon.

Flyers can also be an excellent source of finding undervalued properties. By delivering flyers to thousands of mailboxes in various neighborhoods over a period of time, you will more than likely get some good responses. Also give flyers to real estate agents, property managers, and anyone else who may be a potential "bird dog." Here's an example of a particularly effective sign/flyer:

DO YOU WANT IMMEDIATE CASH FOR YOUR HOME?
HOME CAN BE IN ANY AREA & IN ANY CONDITION!
CALL ROBERT SHEMIN RIGHT NOW!!
000-0000.
We guarantee results quickly and safely.
We can close in 24 hours if needed.

Local "shoppers" and neighborhood papers can be an excellent place to put your ads. Also, use billboards at grocery stores, churches, and community centers for your flyers. Advertise yourself. Tell everyone you meet that you buy houses. Print up business cards that say, "I buy houses" or "I'll pay cash for your house." Distribute as many cards as possible.

Flyers

Advantages: **You will find some good deals. This method keeps your name and number out among the public.**

Disadvantages: Advertising can be expensive. Response to advertising is hit or miss; sometimes people call you, sometimes they don't. Find the most cost-efficient way to advertise (that does not mean the cheapest). Negotiate with your newspaper or direct mail company. You can do a lot of it yourself—direct mail, flyers, bulletin boards, and business cards.

8. REAL ESTATE AGENTS.

When I started out, I used real estate agents. They can be excellent sources of information about how to find and acquire undervalued properties. They have access to all of the homes that are listed for sale through agents in your area. They can be an excellent source of market information, financing tools, and lists of foreclosures.

If possible, *tell every single real estate agent* in your area that you are an investor looking for undervalued properties (give them a price range). Why? Real estate agents make a commission off of every house they sell, so they're always looking for buyers. Real estate agents may prove to be some of your best "bird dogs." Although most of the deals they will present to you will not be "deals," thank them for calling you and encourage them to call again. Soon enough, one of these agents will present you with the right deal. Do not be afraid to contact every single agent in town— let them work for you.

Many real estate agents have access to computers and books called the Multiple Listing Service (**MLS**). The MLS is a directory of all houses listed (through agents) for sale. Through these resources, agents can narrow a search and find properties that you are looking for, i. e., nonqualifying loans, fixer-uppers, etc. They can also help you determine the true value of these properties through the use of comparable sales of other properties in the neighborhood.

Please remember that even though a property may be listed with a real estate agent, the real estate agent's true job (and *only* job) is to carry offers to the seller. Therefore, never hesitate or feel timid about making a low offer, even if it's to an agent. The agent may laugh and look at you funny; but again, the agent must carry the offer to the seller, no matter how ludicrous it may be.

In sum, real estate agents can be an excellent source of locating properties and determining the value of properties; and, down the road, they can be an excellent source for selling the properties.

Real Estate Agents

Advantages: **Real estate agents are excellent sources of good deals and good market information. Many specialize in working with investors like you and can** find nonqualifying or owner's terms properties.

Disadvantages: Agents get commissions which must come from the sales price, thus increasing your costs. Make sure you know who the agent represents. Most of the time, they represent the seller. You may want to think about becoming an agent yourself to get part of the commission.

> ## Robert's Rule: Don't Allow Your Contract to Be Shopped
>
> When you put a purchase agreement on a property, whether it's through an agent or the owner, *never* allow your contract to be "shopped." It is illegal for a real estate agent to do it and you can lose many good deals, too.
>
> *What is "shopping a contract"?* Suppose you submit a purchase agreement on a property, and instead of accepting, rejecting, or making a counter-offer, the realtor holds the contract and calls other potential buyers. Typically, the realtor (or whoever) will ask other buyers, "I've got a contract on 100 Main Street for $30,000, can you offer more?
>
> *How can you protect yourself?* Always insist on writing into the contract that the offer will expire and be voided in 24 hours, two days, five days, or whatever you choose. Make sure the sellers and/or their agent understand that you have other good deals and you cannot wait long for an answer. If you ever believe that a realtor has shopped your contract, please report the person to your local Board of Realtors and/or the person's boss.

9. REAL ESTATE INVESTMENT ASSOCIATIONS.

Most major cities have a real estate investment club. These are organizations of real estate investors that get together every few weeks and trade investment ideas. They let each other know what properties they have for sale, what they're looking for, tips on how to find properties or to be a better landlord, etc. These clubs are excellent places to meet other people in real estate and find properties that may be a very good deal for you. The knowledge, education and camaraderie you will gain from these clubs, along with the possibility of finding really good properties, must not be overlooked. Find out if there is a real estate investment club in your area and/or consult our list of real estate investment club—and if there is one near you, please join.

Real Estate Investment Associations

Advantages: **Great way to meet other investors, contractors, buyers, and sellers. Learn a lot of good information. Find a mentor.**
Disadvantages: **None.**

10. ATTORNEYS AND CPAs.

Since foreclosures, estate sales, and divorces can be good sources of great real estate deals, you should contact as many attorneys as possible and let them know that you buy real estate. It's important to find out who the big foreclosure attorneys are in your area and try to set up meetings with them. Constantly remind them that you buy. They may also be able to put you in contact with lending institutions that are foreclosing on property.

It is possible that these attorneys and lending institutions already let their friends or other investors know about the "good deals." Make yourself one of these people. Take the attorneys out to lunch, send short thank-you letters. Be advised, however, of the attorney ethics rules (yes, some attorneys have ethics!). Some attorneys may not be able to tell you anything, depending upon the circumstances, because they have to protect their clients' identities.

In addition, accountants or CPAs may be a good source of real estate deals. They may know of other investors or special situations (divorces, estate sales, people in financial trouble who may need to sell).

Robert's Rule:

If you are to become a serious real estate investor you need access to a good real estate attorney and CPA.

Shop around and find someone who is active in real estate. Not only will that person be an excellent and much-needed advisor to your business, but probably a source of deals as well.

Building Your Network List.

Most of my best deals have come from others in real estate who know that I'm buying—other investors like myself. They, too, are out there uncovering good deals. Sometimes these investors just might lack the necessary funds to buy a really solid deal. To make sure they don't miss a profit opportunity, they will call you to take advantage of the deal and take a commission or finder's fee.

Your most precious asset is your list of prospective buyers.

Begin immediately to compile a list of prospective buyers. Believe me, everything from this point on in your career starts with compiling a prospect list. Do that, and you can take virtually any real estate business and—by regularly mailing offers and information and telemarketing to your list—double or triple your profits in a matter of six months.

Truth be known, I've heard every excuse under the sun for why most real estate people fail to start the compilation process. I've concluded that the single biggest enemy is inertia. No one can get you to succeed in spite of yourself.

Every time you meet a real estate agent, see an ad in the newspaper, have someone respond to an ad, bump into a likely prospect at an auction, meet real estate club members, visit attorneys who specialize in real estate, meet accountants, learn of a group of home buyers, etc. —get names, addresses, and phone numbers and put the information on your computer. In other words, begin to identify (for future use) the most probable prospects in your area in a comprehensive list. You'll see later just how critical to your success this will be.

Let's take a minute and discuss the incredible importance of this list. Someone on your list might be thinking seriously of moving. Or perhaps you've sold that person a property before and have thereby gained trust. Or maybe a prospect can put you in touch with a friend or relative who's interested in buying a piece of real estate. Maybe someone wants to sell an existing house. Another may be in the process of a divorce proceeding and need to sell a house quickly. Perhaps as part of a settlement a husband or wife has to get rid of a house. Or maybe a relative died and the estate wants to unload some properties quickly. Maybe a prospect on your list has reached an age when he wants to be a passive investor.

The point here is that if you keep in regular contact with these people, you can have a customer for life. But you can't have any of this unless you begin to compile a prospect list. If you do, you can compete with the best real estate pro on the planet—and end up the winner.

The Most Effective Letter to Locate Properties

This letter can easily be adapted to locate buyers or investors as well.

Honest Profits

[Note: This letter must be followed up three to four days later with a telephone call. And the telephone script will follow.]

This letter should be personally typed with a word processor. I generally attach a dollar bill to the top of the letter—although from time to time I will attach a bright shiny penny instead. The letter goes like this:

Dollar bill/penny attached to letter

Dear Mr. Jones,

As you can see, I have attached a brand new dollar to the top of this letter. Why have I done this? Fact is, there are two reasons:

#1. I have something extremely important to tell you and I needed some way to be absolutely certain this letter catches your attention.

#2. And second, since what I am writing about can make you a great deal of money, I thought using a dollar bill as a financial eye-catcher was quite appropriate.

Here's what it's all about:

At this point, you complete the letter by revealing what the benefits are of doing business with you. Here are some examples:
- I understand that you have a For Sale By Owner piece of property that you are attempting to sell yourself.
- I understand that you have a distressed piece of property you are trying to sell.
- I understand that you have invested in distressed property in the past. I have two excellent duplexes that I believe are tremendous investments. I also believe I can structure a venture that will net you, at the very least, $10,000, but more likely $15,000 to $25,000 in bottom line profits. Plus, I'm willing to take the bulk of the risk.

Letter to an Attorney Specializing in Real Estate

> Dear _____,
>
> My name is Robert Shemin, and I have a proposition for you that can quite possibly bring you in more clients. Fact is, if you've been looking for an effective and yet low-key way to market your services and improve the visibility of your practice perhaps I can be of assistance.
>
> I specialize in locating and rehabilitating distressed property.
>
> My service in the community is a well-accepted fact, since I have a successful track record in the low- and mid-income area that few real estate people get involved with.
>
> I'm looking to have a longstanding relationship with an attorney who comes into contact with the types of properties that I am seeking. If you are that attorney, I would like to set up an appointment with you at your convenience.
>
> I will have my secretary call you in the next few days to set up a meeting. For both of our benefits, I hope you will avail yourself of this splendid opportunity.
>
> Sincerely,
>
> Your Name

Second Step:

Three days later, telephone the prospect and say, "Hello, Mr. Jones? This is Robert Shemin. Did you receive a letter recently with a dollar bill attached to it? You did? Good. I just wanted to check and see if you received it. You can't always trust the mail service these days. Isn't that right?

[Note: That's two yes responses you've received!] I just want to ask you if the dollar bill was still attached when you received it? It was? Great. "

[Note: That's the third "yes"!] At this point you can merely ask if he/she would like to set up a date and time to discuss your proposal.

LETTER TO REAL ESTATE CLUB MEMBERS

My advice is to join the most popular real estate club in your area. Once you've met several of the members and you have a piece of property to sell, get this letter out. To really hedge your bet on a piece of property in advance of purchase (e. g., once you have an option on the house), this letter can be a true litmus test to determine if you have a real winner.

Right Of First Refusal

Dear Valued Club Member,

As a courtesy to members of the Nashville Real Estate Club, I am writing you this advance notification of my intent to sell an exceptional piece of property that I have recently rehabbed.

I am extending the Right of First Refusal to those of you who might have an interest—in advance of knowledge to any other investors.

If you want to avail yourself of this quite remarkable investment opportunity, I suggest you contact me rather quickly at 000-0000.

I am extending this Right of First Refusal to you because I believe (from previous conversations with several club members) that the property is essentially what you are seeking.

On the next page is a description of the property. If you have a serious interest, please call my secretary to schedule a meeting.

Sincerely,

Your Name

P. S. I've seen it time after time. Some will take a "wait and see" approach, while others will act now and make money while they are sitting and watching from the sidelines.

How the Professionals Find Undervalued Properties

**Letter to Tap into an Attorney's, Accountant's,
Financial Planner's Client Base**

(To seek prospects that have an interest in real estate investments)

Dear _____,

You probably have clients who are seeking safe, secure real estate investments. And perhaps it would be to their benefit if you were to point these unique investments out. I'm talking about investments that take the guesswork out of real estate property ownership.

If you would like, I would be happy to have lunch or a cup of coffee with you to share some rather unique ideas. I would be happy to show you a number of properties that I believe are exceptional values. I would do this solely as a service to you and your clients.

Obviously tapping into my client base could be a way to improve the marketing of your professional services as well, which I will also be happy to discuss with you.

For my part, I am looking for a long and enduring relationship— one based on your and your clients' needs. I will not simply show you the kinds of properties that would be in my self-interest to sell.

I think you'll find that I am quite knowledgeable in the field and do uncover exceptional values from time to time. And when I discover an uncommon value, I'll merely ask you if it is something your clients really are interested in.

I can't be any fairer than that. Because we both have a complex schedule, I will give you a call in a few days and see if we can find an available free moment to get together.

Sincerely,

Your Name

P. S. Our meeting may change your entire thinking about real estate investments and how to identify and bring in new clients. And it may change your client's ideas on how to obtain alternate financing for specific projects. My business has grown rapidly because of this type of information, and I would appreciate the time to share them with you.

Here then is a summary of how to locate solid deals:

1. Check your local newspaper (Saturday and Sunday editions are best) and locate properties with potential to rehabilitate.

Important: If possible, concentrate your efforts in one or two neighborhoods that have the most buying (and selling) activity.

　a. Look for areas where the homes are all essentially similar in construction.

This way it is easier to compare homes and establish a value.

b. Look for homes that were built after 1945. Be careful of homes that have been painted with lead as an ingredient. The cost to remove any lead may have to be figured into your projections.

c. Look out for homes in the area that are particularly run down. Check the backyards. Is the neighborhood near a school? Look for the most unattractive and most physicallywanting-of-repairs type home. This is the easiest type of home in which to do cosmetic (often not costly) surgery. Sometimes just calling in a painter, adding a few ceiling fans or some mortar, and enlisting a lawn service can do wonders to fix up a drab and dingy home—and give you a sizable appreciation in value.

2. Look for "For Sale By Owner" (FSBO) homes that are in poor shape. If you are looking for owner-financing situations, this can be an excellent source. Compile a list by address and send each one a letter every month.

3. Look for "For Rent By Owner" homes. From time to time an owner has given up on renting and is in an unhappy financial and mental position—and ready to sell the property. This can be yet another good source of owner financing.

Robert's Rule:

The first key to negotiating the purchase of a home is to determine exactly how motivated a seller is to "unload" the property. If you do not have a motivated seller, you probably do not have a good deal. To quickly determine the anxiety index of the seller (and to construct a shockproof real estate portfolio), make sure you uncover the following information:

- Why is this person selling the house?
- What will the seller do with the proceeds?
- Are owner's terms possible?
- For what period of time has the property been on the market?
- Is there a time frame in which the property must be sold?
- Is the owner in financial trouble?
- What will happen to the property if it is not sold?
- What type of neighborhood is it in?

4. Sale due to nonpayment of back taxes is another type of sale to target. Check with your local courthouse. It is true, however, that many states have a debtor

redemption period that goes into effect whereby the debtor can take back the property if the debt is paid within a specified period.

So be careful and check your local laws—and ask an attorney for help.

5. Estate sales. These are also an excellent source to target. Simply stay in regular contact with attorneys in your area who specialize in this area. (Get a list from the Bar Association.) From time to time, family needs and conflicts necessitate a quick sale of an estate. It's also a good idea to stay in touch with the probate agency in your city to determine the estate executor on file.

6. Foreclosures. Check your local paper (or check with your attorney) under "Legal Notices." You just may be able to purchase the property slightly in advance of foreclosure by assuming the loan and purchasing the debt. If you wait for foreclosure, cash is king.

Most foreclosures bought on the courthouse steps require cash or a cashier's check from a bank.

7. Vacant homes. Make it a daily ritual to look for properties that are vacant. Get out of your car and check the property out. You can determine the owner by simply contacting your local tax agency.

8. Realtors. Make your needs known to the most active realtors in your area. Introduce yourself and say, "I'm looking to invest in properties. And what I'm looking for are physically rundown properties that are livable but that will take a bit of cosmetic surgery to bring in a solid profit." Let as many real estate agents as possible know that you are looking for good deals on wholesale homes. Ask them their fee and the best way to work with them. Then call them back on a regular basis.

9. One-on-one prospecting. This entails not only calling on friends and referrals, but getting out on the street and knocking on doors. It means calling on banks, S&Ls, finance firms, and credit unions to determine if they own particular properties they want to sell. It means approaching attorneys, accountants, and financial planners to determine if they have clients in need. It means calling on builders who have either gone "belly up" or are under financial pressure to sell (it is also possible that some builders have incomplete homes or trade-ins they want to salvage).

10. Auctions. The first thing to do is to check your Yellow Page listings under Auctions. Call state auction firms, get placed on their mailing list and begin attending. You'll begin to make some excellent contacts.

11. FHA. and VA repos. When a borrower defaults on financing, the FHA or the VA buys the mortgage from the lender. These agencies then make every effort to resell the property. Contact the HUD. Regional Federal Housing Office or your Regional VA Housing Agency and obtain a list of their repossessions. Look in your Sunday real estate section or ask a realtor.

Honest Profits

12. Ads, telemarketing, and direct mail. What you are looking for here is a direct mail piece or an ad that encourages the target prospect to call you.

a. Compile a list of "For Sale By Owner" names and addresses. Then mail the prospect a letter, and follow up with a telephone call at least three days later.

b. Another direct mail/telemarketing method that works is to get a list of absentee owners and simply mail them a letter telling them what you are after. You can obtain a list of all property owners from your local property tax office. Search for owners' addresses that are NOT the exact property address provided on the list (this means that the property is probably investment property). Also try to find out if there is one section in your area that has more buying and selling activity than others. It is a good idea to concentrate your direct mail efforts initially in these areas.

c. Hire several "commission only" telemarketing people (part-time housewives/college students) and have them follow up on your direct mail letters and call prospects and tell people about your services, tapes, and exactly how you can meet their needs. Always educate and caringly inform.

13. Get leads from competitors. By attending auctions and contacting your competitors you will be surprised at the number of leads that can become available.

14. Offer finders' fees to "bird dogs": contractors, handymen, mailmen, carpet cleaners, roofing and siding reps, landscapers, movers, and anyone who comes into contact with your prospects for leads. Be sure to make it worth their while. A simple letter can often do the job. This is hardly different from getting commissioned salespeople to help pay for your advertising and marketing program. You can also offer to reciprocate by providing the finders with your leads. You can also offer to buy leads for $2 a lead and offer a commission of $250—$500 for each lead that results in a closing. That proposition can get everyone's attention.

Remember: Good marketing is nothing more than salesmanship multiplied.

15. Real estate investment clubs. One way to achieve your goal is to contact prospects with the same interest, or those who subscribe to specific publications or organizations. Since many of these people own real estate, they are likely prospects. Call the association or organization, ask to rent the list, and make a simple mailing—or simply attend the meetings and introduce yourself.

16. Friends. Don't overlook contacting people you know. They can be a rich source of leads.

Let them know what you are looking for—and don't forget to pay them a finder's fee. Then they'll always be looking for homes for you.

17. Property managers can be an excellent source of leads because they probably already have properties they would like to get rid of or know of owners who want to sell. Do a mass mailing followed up with a phone call to all local property management

firms.

18. Out-of-town owners. Compile a list of these owners and send them a direct mail letter. Follow it up with a telephone call three to four days later.

19. Seminars. Holding seminars entails renting a room at a well-located public library. In your ads and direct mail piece, offer to educate your prospect FREE by offering a seminar on "What to Do to Get More Money if You're Thinking of Selling Your House," or "Can You Make More Money Selling Your House Yourself?" or "How to Get Top Equity Out of Your House!" or "How to Package Your Loan Fast!" You can also bring in different speakers (bankers, mortgage firms, etc.) willing to talk about subjects of interest (e. g., loans, refinancing, how to buy more property by trading your existing home, saving money on points, joint venture investing, free evaluation) to your prospects. You can tell attendees that "If you qualify we can buy your home in one day flat and we will turn-key the entire project for you."

Important: What you want to develop is an active, ongoing action marketing plan that includes direct mail, telemarketing, seminars, and counseling services. You want to keep experimenting with different ads, letters, and telemarketing strategies. What you're looking for is not how many prospects respond, but how many properties you actually close on. This means that if you spend $60 every week on mailings to 100 people, and there are 1,000 prospects in your area, and you get a 2% response—you have twenty new prospects over every ten-week period.

By the way, you can generally double your response rate if you telemarket to your list three to four days after you have made your mailing. The point: You can either continue mailing to the list (if your mailing piece is effective) or try a different approach. In any event, it's the number of leads that convert that you are interested in.

CHAPTER 2

Money: You May Not Have It, But You'd Better Know Where to Find It!

*The winners in life think constantly in terms of
I can, I will and I am.
Losers, on the other hand,
concentrate their waking thoughts
on what they should have or would have done, or what they can't do.*
Dr. Dennis Waitley

Some people sit and watch the world go by—and it does.
Anonymous

Almost every real estate investment seminar, book, and television infomercial promises that if you follow their program, you can become a "millionaire even if you have no money." Is this really true? It is possible, but you're going to have to work night and day and kick and claw and scratch your way up the ladder. You don't need to do that, however. There actually are ways to attract capital to your real estate investment business.

Let me explain. You found a deal. Now how do you buy it? Finding deals can be easy; finding the money can be difficult. So now, read on to learn just about every possible way to find money...

Bank Financing.

The most difficult way to borrow money is from a bank. A few years ago banks were not loaning money on investment property, but they're doing a bit more now. When it comes to borrowing money from a bank, though, it's a Catch 22 situation.

Banks require that you have a track record, a good credit history, and the ability to put up some of your own money. Many people cannot meet these requirements.

Honest Profits

Nevertheless, it is quite possible to borrow money from a bank.

Assuming you have established a good relationship with a bank and you have a decent credit history, you should be able to find a bank to lend you money. Here's how. You need to prepare a powerful **Benefits Package** that will knock their socks off.

A Benefits Package is a detailed business plan which includes exactly what you want to do—actual property prospects and financial data on the property, your business mission, your resume, and all other important financial data. Include two years of tax returns, a completed and updated financial statement, and a copy of your credit report (which you can request from your local credit reporting agency).

I've enclosed a sample Benefits Package in the Appendix entitled Ramsey Avenue Duplex Project. The Ramsey Duplex Project is not a theoretical case. It is an actual Benefits Package I presented to a bank; it describes the specific investment results I intended to achieve. Obviously, such a package should show that there is a high probability you will achieve great returns—especially if you can show that you will be purchasing the property at 40% off retail or better. You should also provide pictures, maps, lot description, a business plan, and so forth.

You must provide lenders with organized data. Actually, the more supporting documents you provide the better. They're going to want tax returns, financial statements and a detailed analysis of the property. You must show what you're buying, that the risk is low, what the market value will be once it has been renovated, what the property will rent for (if you're renting it out), vacancy and repair expense, and what you're going to net. Plus, have pictures, pictures, pictures—in color. Preferably include before and after pictures of other houses you may have renovated.

Another key to borrowing money is to play banks or mortgage companies against each other. Tell every institution that you are indeed "shopping"—talking with two or three lenders. It's amazing what a little competition will do. Tell each of the lenders that, "Yes, I've been led to believe that I will get the loan I'm seeking. I'm just trying to see if I can get a better deal from someone else." Absolutely avoid misrepresentation.

Today, banks are under tremendous pressure to provide Community Reinvestment Act (CRA) money. They're required to invest money in low-income neighborhoods in order to get credit from the federal government. That is, they provide money that will be used for affordable housing to low-income families. Banks now have an incentive and a willingness to expend money and take more risk to renovate specific neighborhoods.

If you are just starting out, or you have bad credit, you may not be able to get a bank loan. But don't fret; there are other ways to find cash.

"Owner's Terms."

If you can't get the funds you're looking for from a bank, some sellers will give you financing. Sometimes a desperate seller will offer you terms on an irresistible basis. If you lack money you can begin by buying real estate on owner's terms.

> # Robert's Rule:
>
> Always, always ask for owner's terms.
>
> Almost all sellers will say that they want cash.
>
> Obtaining owner's terms is still possible—if you can negotiate.
>
> If sellers demand cash, ask them, "Why?"
>
> Usually they will tell you. Ask them what their plans are for the cash.
>
> If they need to pay off a small debt, then ask what they are going to do with the remainder.
>
> If they tell you that they are going to invest it—ask them how much they plan to make on their money.
>
> Perhaps they can earn 6—8%.
>
> Your response to this is: "How would you like to pay off your debt and earn 9—10% with a safe investment?"
>
> They should be interested because it meets their needs.
>
> You can then offer them $3,000 cash down with owner's terms for the balance over 20, 25, 30 years at 9—10% interest.
>
> If you don't have good credit, it's the easiest way to get financing.
>
> Even if you have good credit, you'll probably end up with a better deal on owner's terms.

Nonqualifying Assumable Loans.

There are always a few nonqualifying assumable loans available in the marketplace. Nonqualifying assumable means that anyone can assume them. They're like gold. But they're not easy to uncover. There are some old ones, e. g., FHA and VA loans originating before 1985 or 1986, and some even older. If you can spot one and the property is overleveraged, it can be a genuinely great deal.

Partnering Deals and Investors.

If you have little or no money, you probably need to find partners and/or investors. Relatives, friends, employers, retirees who earn little returns on their money—all may be good sources of money for you. If you find a property that is a good deal, draw up a business plan for it and present it to anyone and everyone that could possibly help you.

1. *Flipping* (to be discussed in detail later): Since you found the deal and you're going to do all of the work to make sure the deal gets done, make an offer to your partner that if he will put up the money, you will split the profits with him 50/50. Always pay your investor back 100% of their investment money first. If there is a profit on the house, then split it up and pay them quickly. By paying the investors back their initial investment before any profits are split up, you'll make them happy to do business with you again.

2. *High return:* You can simply borrow the money from someone else and promise a good return on the money. Perhaps you can find someone who is only getting 5—6% on money in savings accounts, CDs, bonds, etc., and tell that person that you could offer 9 or even 10% on the same money. If you are finding truly undervalued properties, then you can offer your investors a very safe first mortgage. Example: If

Typical Ad

Earn up to 12% on your money!

Very secure investment.

Call or write for more information.

Real and Safe!

(Your phone number.)

Money: . . . You'd Better Know Where to Find It!

the property you found is worth $60,000 retail and you can buy it and fix it up for a total of $40,000 *and* you can prove to your investors that this is true (show them sales of similar homes in the neighborhood and compare them to yours), you can offer them an extremely safe mortgage with an equity cushion of $20,000. Many very successful real estate entrepreneurs began this way. Some investors I know of have raised hundreds of thousands of dollars.

If you don't know anybody who has this type of money, you'll need to start networking with accountants, lawyers, retirees, investment advisors, and older real estate entrepreneurs (who simply don't have the legs to keep running around finding deals). You can also advertise in newspapers.

Robert's Rule:

If you work with partners or investors, always pay them more than they expect.

Why?

Look at it from the investor's viewpoint.

If you promise the investor 10% on his money and then you pay him 11—12%, explaining that you made so much money on this deal you wanted to share it, do you think he'll want to do business with you again?

Of course he will!

And repeat business is what you're after—not the one-time killing.

If you flip or rehab a property and make $15,000 once you sell it, why not give the investor an extra $1,000 after your 50/50 split. Tell him it's a "kicker" or a bonus for working with you. And if you break down the return on his money over a 12-month period, I think he'll be glad to do business with you again. He may even tell his friends, relatives, and business partners to lend money to you.

Develop joint-venture relationships with relatives, friends, contractors, nonprofits, church groups, whomever.

Send a one- or two-page monthly newsletter to prospective investors. Keep them current and explain the life of your investments, the tax consequences, leasing, and so on.

Here are other options for borrowing money that are available to you.

a. Local commercial banks. If you already have a relationship with a bank, it's a good idea to approach your bank contact first.

b. Credit unions. Contact all credit unions in your area and ask for details concerning application.

c. Savings and loans. Obtain information concerning their involvement in the **Community Reinvestment Act (CRA)** which requires particular banks and S & Ls to provide specific community services. A rehab project you are considering purchasing might fall into this category.

All banks must comply with CRA.

d. Equity lines. You can use the equity in your house to borrow money to begin. These can be very attractive loans; but be careful—you don't want to lose your house.

e. Owner or seller financing. This is a creative method of financing whereby the seller finances your purchase of his property. The seller, however, holds clear title and the mortgage on the property until you have paid off the mortgage.

f. Finance companies often charge higher than normal interest rates, and therefore should be your choice of last resort. They offer a good way to get in over your head.

g. Partnerships. Find investors (friends, relatives, etc.) who have investment money. Offer them great returns on their money (10 - 20%). Offer them a first mortgage on the property so that, should anything go wrong, at least they'll be able to get their money out from the sale of the property. To sweeten the deal, you may have to offer them a percentage of the profits as well.

h. Government grants. There are HUD and other government grant programs available. Contact your local housing authority to determine how it functions and how you can qualify.

i. Barter. Offer to barter goods or services with the owner for the down payment on the property. If you manufacture an item such as furniture, a boat or whatever, you can offer a direct exchange of your goods as a down payment. Just make sure you trade for retail value. You can also issue a credit to the seller for an unlimited time.

j. Credit cards. You can borrow money by using your credit cards. Interest rates are exhorbitant. But if you are certain you can flip a property quickly prior to closing, you may want to risk it. This is very risky, so you'd better be absolutely and positively sure that your deal is going to work.

k. Joint venture with the seller.

l. Refinance your existing mortgage. Or you can obtain a home equity loan (a second mortgage with flexible terms) .

m. Cash value in ordinary life insurance. If the policy has been in existence for six years or longer you can qualify for a low-interest rate.

n. Interest on margin loans. Money from a brokerage house. If you own stocks, bonds, or any other marketable security, you can borrow money from a brokerage house on those securities.

o. Place an ad in your newspaper. (I've known people to take out an ad in the newspaper stating, "You'll be secured by a first deed of trust or a first lien on the piece of real estate. It's worth $50,000. I want to borrow $30,000 at such-and-such an interest rate."

Important: Analyze the details of every financing source and make absolutely certain in your cash-flow projections that the terms do not place an unbearable burden on your business plan.

Prefinancing DOs—before you attempt to borrow money:
a. Do get an appraisal.
b. Do get an accurate survey report of property
c. Do get a termite report.
d. Do test wells and septic tanks
e. Have all insurance in place and up to date.

How to Get Banks to Participate in Your Investments.
a. Develop a personal and long-term relationship with at least two bankers. Let them know your personal philosophy. Back that up with a history of a solid credit rating.

b. Initially, try to avoid having numerous credit lines. Be aware of the 28:34 rule that many bankers live by; i. e., mortgage payments, including real estate taxes, should be approximately 28% of an individual's gross monthly salary. And an individual should be spending no more than 34% of his or her gross salary per month on all other debts.

c. Provide the bank with "more than they want to know" about your potential investment in the form of an in-depth business plan for the property you intend to purchase.

d. Let the bank know that other banks are interested in loaning you money. Play the banks off one another when negotiating the deal.

e. Call your banker at least once a month and remind him or her that your disciplined and detailed business plan is in operation and progressing smoothly and that you are limiting the use of their money for the single purpose intended in your business plan.

Honest Profits

Banks rarely hear from their customers. They'll appreciate the professionalism that you bring to the deal.

f. Remember that the primary objective of a bank (and responsibility to its shareholders) is to make safe and secure loans.

g. Make sure you compare the interest rates you are offered with other financial institutions in your area. Remember: Everything is negotiable. Everything. That includes interest rates, points, fees, terms, you name it!

Check the terms of every loan agreement you are offered—not only the interest payments, the insurance, the balloon and any escape clauses (that allow the lender to escape from low interest rates they've offered), but every detail in the contract, including the penalty if you cannot make a payment. And remember, always negotiate, negotiate, negotiate.

How to Design a Successful Financing Package for the Lending Institution.

Make sure you design a professionally organized financing package (have an accountant review the numbers and make sure to present the package in a very professional format). Included in the package should be the following:

Your bank package should include:

1) A nice title page.
　　Example: "Loan Request for _____ (your name)
　　　　Presented to _____ (your bank). "
2) A mission statement.
　　Example: To profitably buy, rehabilitate, and sell homes in _____(your city) which will benefit the community and provide much-needed, quality, affordable housing to first-time home buyers. "
3) A brief, professional-sounding short- and long-term business plan (one to two pages) .
4) Your resume.
5) Your financial statement. A copy of one is in the Appendix.
6) The subject property you want to borrow against.
7) Deatils of your loan request (see Appendix) .
8) A picture of the property.
9) A map showing the property's location.
10) A copy of your credit report (you can request one from your local credit-reporting agency) .

11) Two years of your tax returns.
12) An executive summary of you and your loan request, stressing benefits to the bank.
13) At least six references.
14) Cash flow projections and analysis.
15) Projected ROI
(Return on Investment).
16) Show the demand for the investment property
17) If possible, list your past successes in converting homes
and provide income-expense statements on each property.
Note: See Forms for a sample bank proposal

Here Are More Financing Options:

1) Assumable mortgage. The buyer assumes the responsibility for the payments (the difference between the sale price and the balance owed) on the seller's existing mortgage. This is the way to go if you have available cash and want to benefit from a lower interest rate—and if you want to avoid closing costs. Another plus is that under this scenario you may not have to qualify. But some lenders still require a buyer to qualify. Lenders can also increase your interest rate on the assumption. (There is no need to qualify on FHA or VA assumable mortgages, nor will these agencies boost interest rates.) Be aware that a seller with a low interest rate can ask a higher price for the property. Note: Many pre-1986 mortgages are assumable nonqualifying. Post-1986 mortgages are mostly qualifying assumable or are not assumable.

2) Contract for deed. In this case the seller retains the title to the property until the buyer meets the complete terms of the contract. The buyer has to provide a down payment on the property and pay the monthly balance. This is also called a Contract for Sale or a Land Contract. This is excellent if you want to leverage your cash or if you can't qualify for a loan. Watch out, though, because the seller could fail to deliver a clear title due to a divorce, tax lien, etc.

You can use a third party, attorney, CPA, or friend to make sure all of the taxes and insurance are paid.

3) Second mortgage. In the event of a default, a second mortgage is junior (or second) to another senior (or first) mortgage that has first repayment right to an outstanding balance. This is the reason second mortgage holders often receive a higher rate of interest. A second mortgage is an excellent instrument if you lack sufficient cash to buy a property. You can also use a second mortgage if interest rates are too high or hard to get, or you want to purchase a higher priced property from a motivated owner. Remember: The term of the loan is shorter on seconds, so payments could be

Honest Profits

larger. Second mortgages frequently are not permissible on FHA or high-percentage financing arrangements.

4) Seller financing. This is for the seller who wants to earn more money by providing the financing when money is hard to obtain or finding a buyer is difficult. The buyer merely provides a note (secured by a second deed of trust). It is also for the owner who has little or no balance remaining on the property. This is often an excellent situation if you are the buyer, because no outside lender is required and you do not have to qualify or put down a large cash payment. In some cases, a buyer can also obtain better terms and interest rates simply because the owner is anxious to sell in a slow market. Note: Always ask for "owner's terms" or owner's financing before you seek any other type of financing arrangement. Be creative. For example, you can offer to fix up a property that needs work and share the profits with the seller when the property is sold. That is, if you get a contract for $40,000 on the house and put $5,000 into it to fix it up, and then sell it for $60,000, both you and the seller will be happy splitting up the profits. Actually, many new investors get started this way.

5) Lease option agreement. In a lease purchase agreement, you will have to sign a lease and sales contract at the same time. The reason: The lease is utilized initially while the Sales Contract or option comes in to play at a later date. You can use this strategic tool if you lack available cash. This strategy also allows you to lock in a specific price on the property. This is beneficial for the sellers since they no longer have to concern themselves with mortgage payments. Generally, the sellers can ask for a higher price for the property and get it. The downside for the sellers, however, is that they don't receive their money until the sales contract takes effect. It is an easy way for a seller to sidestep a "due on sale" clause (the clause in most mortgages stating that when the property is sold the mortgage is "accelerated" or becomes all due and payable).

Note: If a mortgage contains a due on sale clause, it is likely NOT assumable.

If there is a due on sale clause, try using a contract for deed.

6) Wrap-around Mortgage. Also called an "all-inclusive mortgage" (AIM) or an "all-inclusive trust deed" (AITD), a wrap-around mortgage is quite similar to a second mortgage. In this case a buyer can take title, which involves a combined payment consisting of one mortgage (a first) and a "wrap" which includes the first. For safety's sake (since the seller will know precisely when a buyer stops making payments), the seller can keep the first mortgage and make payments from the monies paid on the wrap. The wrap is frequently used on FHA or VA mortgages. In all other respects it is the same as a contract for deed, and can be used if you do not have a sufficient down payment or are unable to qualify for new financing. It can give you an opportunity to purchase a property at a lower interest rate than the current market. The problem:

Many lenders will not allow a wrap (the FHA and VA will), since they require a clause in the contract stipulating a continual interest rate escalator. The advantage to the seller is safety. In addition, the seller can earn more money on a wrap due to the difference in interest rates after the property is sold. Note: Some secondary lenders prohibit wraps. It is a good idea to consult with a real estate attorney before you get involved with a wrap.

An example of a wrap mortgage:

Joe owns a house with one 30-year mortgage for $60,000 on it. The monthly payments are $600. Joe has been making payments for 7 years. You negotiate with Joe to buy his house for $1,000 down, and you make the $600 payment to the bank. You have three choices in paying the bank (first mortgage holder). One, you can pay the bank directly (then Joe has to worry about whether you are making payments). Two, you can pay Joe directly and rely on him to pay the bank (the obvious risk arises—nonpayment by Joe). Three, you can contract with a third party (attorney/trustee) to make the payments to the bank.

You then sell the house to Sue for $3,000 down and payments of $800 per month for 30 years (approximately a total cost of $78,000). You wrap the first mortgage; i.e, Sue sends you $800 per month; you send Joe (or his mortgage company) $600 per month; and you keep the $200-per-month difference as your profit. Title passes to the new buyer, whose mortgage is wrapped around the first one.

Most mortgages have a due on sale clause. In that case, get written permission from the holder of the first mortgage. Many real estate investors ignore the due on sale clause, because it is very unlikely the mortgage company will discover the sale as long as the first mortgagee keeps receiving payments.

7) Blanket mortgage. This instrument allows you to use other types of equity as collateral on new financing. If you are having trouble getting qualified and you have other assets, this could allow you to obtain a new mortgage. The caveat: You put your collateralized equity at risk.

A blanket mortgage covers all or more than one of your properties.

8) Graduated Payment Mortgage (GPM) is simply a mortgage with reduced payments initially, and higher future payments on a predetermined schedule. The payment then levels off for the remainder of the 15- or 30-year contract. GPMs are great if you want more property for your money and you are certain your income will increase over the years. Another benefit: A GPM makes it easier to qualify for a larger loan, since first-year payments are lower.

Problem: Negative amortization can occur since the interest you are saving is added to your mortgage. Therefore, you could end up owing a lot more than a simple

15- or 30-year mortgage.

9) Graduated Payment Adjustable Mortgage (GPAM). Same as GPMs above, as payments are reduced initially and gradually increased over regular intervals. Interest rates, however, are adjusted on 3-, 4-, or 5-year intervals. This allows the borrower to make lower payments for a specified number of years and then to accelerate the principal.

10) Pledged account mortgage. Similar to GPAMs above, except that the buyer is required to make a substantial down payment (10%—15%), which is then deposited to a pledged savings account.

11) Variable rate mortgage. As a buyer, your schedule of payments will be indexed and your interest rate adjusted at least once a year. This is attractive to those who are convinced that interest rates will drop in the near future. If the opposite occurs, your payments will go higher.

12) Shared appreciation mortgage. A shared appreciation mortgage is a repayment schedule in which you choose to share any profit (equity appreciation) in the property with the lender when it is sold. In return, the lender will reduce your interest rate below market, and therefore reduce your payment. This is for those who want lower interest rates (and payments) or cannot qualify at existing interest rates. The problem is that as a buyer you will be giving up a portion of your ROI when you sell the property (generally at a specified date).

13) Rollover Mortgage (ROM). In a ROM, you and the lender agree to a repayment term of perhaps 15 or 30 years. The mortgage rate is then renegotiated or rolled over at regular intervals. This is great for the lender if interest rates increase. The buyer can refinance at a later date, however.

14) Renegotiable Rate Mortgage (RRM). This is a form of financing in which the mortgage is renewed at short intervals and interest rates are adjusted to an index. Maximum yearly adjustment is generally .005 (one-half of one) % per year over a 15- or 30-year schedule. This instrument is for those who believe interest rates will head downward.

15) Conventional mortgage. Not insured or guaranteed by the government. This is a mortgage from a bank or S&L, and they have strict qualifying terms. Secondary lenders such as Fannie Mae and Freddie Mac and Ginnie Mae buy up these mortgages (government and conventional) from the primary lenders. The primary lenders make their money on the amount the lender has loaned out (often 5%) and the fee for servicing the loan. They also make money on points and on the interest rate difference.

Most bank financing for investors is done with conventional mortgages.

16) FHA. The FHA is not in the business of lending money on mortgages. They insure mortgages. If you borrow money from a S&L and it's an FHA loan, the

Money: . . . You'd Better Know Where to Find It!

government insures your mortgage payment to the lender. FHA loans are fully assumable. There are no prepayment penalties; but the buyer does have to qualify for the FHA loan, as does the property itself. The disadvantages: There is a maximum loan amount; the borrower must occupy the property; and there's also a mortgage insurance premium.

17) VA mortgages are essentially the same as the FHA program, with the important distinction that the borrower does not have to come up with a down payment.

No Money Down—Difficult, Yet Possible.

Here are most, if not all, of the ways to buy property with little or no money down.

1. Negotiate owner's terms with the seller. Try (and *always* try) to have the seller sell you the property with no money down, with payments to be made monthly.

Example: You find a home that you think is worth $75,000. You negotiate to buy it for $50,000, $0 cash at closing. The seller will pay all closing costs, and you pay $500 a month for 20 years. Sounds great, doesn't it? Well, *the seller would have to be pretty motivated to take a deal like this*. Nevertheless, I've seen it happen.

If the house needs work, explain to the seller that you are going to spend time and money repairing the house—this is like a down payment. Your time and your money are going into the house so that the seller has little risk. In the event that you do not make payments to the seller, the seller gets to take back a home that is much more valuable because you just fixed it up.

In negotiating owner's terms, always ask for the payments to begin as late as possible, with the first payment due in 1 year, 3 months, or at the end of the first month. If you are buying to rent the house out, you can use the first month's rent to pay down your payments to the seller.

2. Trade something you have of value: A car, a boat, tools. Barter anything you may have in place of a down payment. You never know what a seller might need.

3. If the seller demands a down payment, ask the seller to agree to pay it on terms. Example: Seller wants to sell for $100,000. You know it's a great deal but you don't have the down payment. The seller insists on $10,000 down. Offer $11,000, but only if you can pay it over 30, 20, 10, 5, or 1 year(s) .

4. Borrow money from another source for your down payment. Example: Credit lines, home equity lines, relatives, credit cards (careful), life insurance policies, etc.

5. Use the real estate agent's commission. If the seller wants 6-10% down at closing, negotiate with the agent to take the commission over time. At the closing, the seller generally has to pay the commission in cash to the agent. If the agent agrees (you'll be surprised at the agent's flexibility) to take the commission in the form of a

Honest Profits

note, this saves the seller some cash at closing, which can go toward your down payment.

6. Assume the seller's obligations. Instead of making a cash down payment, assume some of the seller's notes and/or obligations. Perhaps the seller has a payment due; offer to make the payment yourself as your down payment.

7. If you are buying a group of properties or land, sell off part of the land/properties for more than you have optioned or contracted for, and then take the proceeds from that sale and make a down payment. Example: You are buying 4 houses for $30,000 per house. You know that they are worth more. You negotiate 60 days to close and you need 10% cash down to close. You flip one of the houses for $50,000 to someone else. At the simultaneous closing, you make your down payment from the $20,000 proceeds you just received on the flip. Yes, it can be done!

8. Partner a deal. If you find a property that is a great deal and you need 10% down to close (which you do not have), persuade a friend or an investor to partner with you. Say that if your partner puts 10% down on the property, then you'll split the profits 50/50 when you flip the house.

Example: You find an apartment building that is worth $250,000 for sale at $150,000. The seller wants 10% down and will carry a note for 20 years at 10% interest (approximate payments of $1,300 per month). The apartment building has 10 units, and each one will rent, on average, for about $450 per month (or $4,500 per month total). You can make $3,200 per month (before some expenses, of course) ! But you don't have the down payment. Tell a friend or an investor about the deal—ask for the $15,000 down payment and offer to make your friend a 50% partner on the deal. In 10 months' time, your partner will make back his/her down payment, and you'll be making $1,600 per month and building equity. And you didn't even put up a dime!

9. If you can get a line of credit from the bank and use it to purchase property. Use the equity in your home to obtain a down payment. You get to pay off the down payment over time at a reasonable rate, and you get an interest reduction on your taxes.

Honest Profits

that's your retirement plan.

Maybe some of you merely want to buy homes and sell them and make immediate profits. Or maybe you want to buy a property, fix it up, and sell it.

Maybe you love fixing up houses.

Without knowing your specific needs and goals you cannot accurately analyze a property. It's also important to know your risk parameters, because real estate can be risky. But there are ways to make it almost risk-free, or as risk-free as is humanly possible. The key is getting accurate information and always buying property at least 30 - 40% below retail. It won't take you too long to discover that accurate information is indeed the key ingredient in the profit equation.

In analyzing a property the first critical questions that should be asked are:

- "Is the property or area hot?" "What do you think the property will sell for?" Ask people in the neighborhood these questions.
- How long has the property been sitting on the market?
- Are property values in the neighborhood going up or down?
- Is the city/neighborhood dying?
- Is it in an area that you feel comfortable traveling in?
- What percent of the homes are owner occupied as opposed to rentals?
- Are there many vacant homes?

You can find answers to these questions by talking to property managers, the police department, church organizations in an area— and, most importantly, the neighbors (they know more than almost any professional, since they know the history of the house in question, why people move, who's getting divorced, who's moving in, what houses in the area sell for, etc.).

Also go to auctions in the neighborhood.

You have to know the value of a property to know if you're looking at a solid deal!

If there are five houses in the neighborhood and they're all in the $80,000 range, I suggest you put down $70,000 as your estimate in your projections. You see, there are some neighborhoods where no one buys houses, except for investors. There are other neighborhoods where people buy anything in almost any condition. You need to know this information.

Here's a fail-safe insider system that I use to determine if a property is hot or not. It's a simple but incredible strategy to know in advance if you have a good deal. Prior to buying a property, run an ad in the newspaper describing it. Pretend you're going to rent or sell the property in question. See who calls you. If no one calls, you've learned that the area is dead. On the other hand, if you suddenly get 100 calls, you've learned that you have a potentially very hot property. This way you won't spend your

What Everyone Ought to Know About Analyzing Properties

> ## *Robert's Rule:*
>
> I usually call or inquire about 40 properties and look at 20 more before I even put a contract down.
> Why? I want to make sure that I'm getting a good deal.

hard-earned cash on a piece of property that won't work.

Ok, so what is a good deal? When you uncover a solid deal there are a number of ways to make money on it.

1. You buy it and hold it. You rent it out; you are the landlord.
2. You buy it. You wholesale it, or sell it to investors. This is called "flipping."
3. You buy it. You fix it up. You sell it to an investor or to a retail buyer. This is called "rehabbing" it.

Many of the good deals that you will find will need some sort of repairs. Though some of my best deals have needed the most amount of work, I recommend that you start with a property that only needs cosmetic work; i. e., consider painting, carpeting and/or redecorating. Why? In the beginning you do not want to be overwhelmed or assume too much risk for a major renovation project.

The two most important variables in deciding whether to buy a property are the *projected expenses* and the *projected sales price* (and if you are renting it out, the *projected rental income*).

The key to buying real estate is that you actually make or lose money *when you buy the property*. What does this mean? It means that if sold the property the day after you bought it, you could sell it for more than you bought it for. But not every deal that you come across will initially look like a great deal. However, negotiated correctly, a deal that once looked bad could turn out to be one of your best deals. This happens to me all the time. Typically, I'll be presented with a deal that makes no sense whatsoever. Rather than hang up the phone, though, I start asking questions to find out what the seller wants out of the deal. Pretty soon, you'll start to see the seller's motivating factors and you may be able to come up with a creative way to make the deal work for both of you.

How to Analyze Properties.

1. To appraise the actual value of the property under current market conditions, do the following:

- Understand up front that the properties you are seeking must have a high profit potential. In almost all cases they will require work in order to bring you the high profit you are looking for. This means that **you must determine in advance the repair costs** to make it a marketable commodity. All the more reason to call a professional appraiser or a home inspector! Also get several bids from trustworthy contractors.

Note: Because so much of your potential future profits are riding on these numbers, I suggest you require a scrutinizing examination by a professional before you go ahead and buy the property. The reason: If your own estimates are in error it can really cost you dearly. Besides, if a professional inspection uncovers costly problems that lie hidden in the property, you can then turn around and show the report to the seller—and ask for a significantly lower price.

- Obtain a list of all the properties in the immediate area and check the price they have actually sold for during the past 3 to 6 months. Begin by calling your real estate agent, the Registrar of Deeds, or your local tax agency. Also find out if the area is presently overvalued or undervalued.

- The next important phase is to match similar homes in the neighborhood with the property you are analyzing. (These are called "comps," or comparable sales.) Compare the square footage and the selling price to estimate the price per square foot; e.g., if the square footage of a somewhat identical home is 1,000 square feet and it sold for $60,000, you can use a price of $60 per square foot as an estimate in your analysis.

- Call in a certified appraiser and get a professional opinion on all the expenses involved in the property in question. Your cost should be in the neighborhood of $200. It can be the best investment you will make. It is a good idea to include this in your loan application if you cannot take over an assumable mortgage.

- Check with your local housing authority (HUD, FHA, VA) to see if special financing (low-interest neighborhood revitalization grants) is available. Plug these numbers into your profit and loss projections.

- Check the zoning laws. It might be possible to convert a residential property to a commercial or mixed-use zone. The difference in rental income can be dramatic. Converting a residential property to one occupied by a medical, dental, or professional office can be extremely lucrative. In any event, check the zoning on all prospective properties. Make absolutely certain of the zoning re-

What Everyone Ought to Know About Analyzing Properties

quirements in advance of any involvement.

- Check with the local police in the area to see if the neighborhood property is safe. Yes, this will have an impact on price and how fast the property gets sold.
- Check your basic assumptions with realtors in your area who are familiar with specific areas. Call lenders and ask their views on the area.
- If the property is an investment property, review the property's profit and loss statement, item by item to understand why the present owner is having financial problems. Know in advance how you are going to solve these problems. Was it divorce, foreclosure possibilities, poor management, financing difficulties, elderly who want out of an area or want to downgrade their lifestyle, a neighborhood in transition, the owners' high life style, unforeseen damage or heavy repair costs, or liens? What is really going on?

More Analysis.

By all means, check out the utilities when you look at a home.

Have the utilities turned on before you buy a property.

I made the mistake of ignoring that advice and it cost me. A lot of first-time owners don't walk through a property with a contractor, thereby missing one of the most critical phases of analyzing a property.

The more times you walk through homes and review expenses the smarter you get. On the plus side, from time to time you'll also discover assets hidden in the property that will allow you to sell that property a lot quicker than you ever thought.

I'm turned on by rundown houses that others have ignored or are avoiding!

It's true. I look for houses that are torn up and have broken windows, filthy carpets, holes in floors, and colors that could make you regurgitate. Some have five feet of trash in the yard, broken fences, window shades in tatters, broken toilet seats, and poor landscaping. Other potential buyers walk in an unmaintained house and say, "Oh, no, it'll cost $30,000 to $50,000 to repair this house. It's a pigpen." That's an emotional response. It's not necessarily logical or true.

Simply walk through the house with a contractor and ask what it will take to turn this poorly maintained home into one in average condition—not beautiful condition, mind you, but AVERAGE CONDITION. You see, you can buy carpet for $4, $5, or $6 a yard installed. Paint is not costly either. I can have a two-bedroom, one-bath duplex painted for approximately $250. And I'm talking a nice paint job.

CHAPTER 4

Controlling, Holding, and Protecting Real Estate

You have now learned all the ways to locate properties and evaluate them to determine if you've truly found a good deal. In this chapter you will learn how to "control" real estate, the secrets of writing great contracts for purchase of real estate, how to title property (that is, in what name or in what form you should take title—one that benefits you the most).

The issues that we will look at concern not only how to write the good contracts, but also the intricacies of effective titling of properties. That is, should you title a property in your name, or in someone else's name? Should you use a corporation or a trust, and what are the implications, advantages, and disadvantages of these methods regarding legal liability and both income tax and estate taxes? Included for your education and enjoyment are samples of real estate contracts. Most real estate agents will be more than glad to provide you with a contract. However, I will teach you certain secrets real estate professionals use, and that you must use, that will benefit you greatly.

The key to "controlling" real estate is: Once you find a good deal, you must **"lock the property up"** as quickly as possible. Why? Unfortunately, you're not the only one looking to find good deals or how to spot them. The name of the game is speed.

How do you lock it up? You need to get a signed Purchase Agreement or an Option Contract on the property. Once you get a signed contract for the sale of real estate, you now control that real estate for as long as the time period or limitations of your contract specify. Find it, put a contract on it, and control it. If you do not do it immediately, someone else will. Keep in mind that a Purchase Agreement and an Option Contract do not convey title to you. These contracts simply state that the seller *will* transfer title to you on a future date, so long as both you and the seller meet the specifications spelled out in the contract. If you "control" it, the seller cannot sell the property out from under you. You, on the other hand, can resell the property prior to the closing date, *if* you follow my instructions below.

Honest Profits

Example:

Not too long ago, I was approached by one of my favorite bird dogs. He told me he had found a really great deal on a house on which the mortgage company had foreclosed. My bird dog learned that the mortgage company was just looking to reclaim its loan balance (the amount of money still owed on the property) out of the sale. The mortgage company was selling the property, regardless of its true value, for the amount of the loan it had on the property. He told me it was a $120,000 house that could be bought for $70,000. Naturally, I did not believe him. It sounded too good to be true.

We went and looked at the house. It was a beautiful, four-bedroom, three-bath home, with a full garage, in good shape. It just needed to be painted inside, and perhaps have some new carpet. It had a pool, almost an acre of land, and was very spacious, very nice, very modern, very well kept, in a beautiful neighborhood of what seemed to be $130,000—$180,000 homes. However, it was in an area that I was not very familiar with. I knew it was a good deal, but I decided to wait a few days and do some more research on the property.

The bird dog had brought me some comparable sales of similar houses in that area that had sold for about $130,000—$150,000; and also, the tax assessor had appraised the house at $135,000. The bird dog told me again that it could be purchased for around $70,000. I waited a few days and did some more research and verified everything that I had been told. Indeed it was a $130—140,000 house. I called my bird dog up and found out that the house had been sold the day that I had looked at it for about $70,000.

That day, I relearned one of the first rules of real estate: "He who hesitates is lost." I hesitated and I lost. When I first looked at the house and thought it was a good deal, I should have locked it up immediately. That is, I should have put a contract on the house to control it. But since I didn't lock it up or put a contract in on it, I had no control of the house and the house was sold to someone else who probably profited greatly from that property.

Let's say you've found what you think might be a great property. What should you do? You need to lock it up right away. Then you need to ask yourself, "Which contract am I going to use to lock it up?" Feel free to use one of the contract samples we have provided for you. **However, you must have it reviewed by a local attorney to make sure that it complies with your state law.** You may also get a sample copy of a real estate contract from your local Board of Realtors, a real estate agent friend, or an attorney friend.

Very often, the seller of the real estate will want to provide his or her own contract. Do not let this bother you, for I often do many things to make the seller feel as comfortable as possible. Then I can get the best deal possible. If the sellers insist on using their contract, go ahead and use it; but you will modify it to best suit your purposes.

The most important thing about negotiating contracts is to understand what it is that the seller really wants or needs. We call this the **"Game of 1000 Polite Questions."** You should try to get answers to the following questions (phrase them in a way that you think is appropriate and nonthreatening):

1. Why are the sellers selling?
2. What are they going to do with the money?
3. Why do they need the money?
4. What are their real reasons for getting rid of the house?
5. How long have they owned the property?
6. Who actually owns it (is it in their name, or someone else's name, a partnership)?
7. How quickly do they want to sell it?
8. How long have they been trying to sell it?
9. How have they tried to sell it?
10. Is there a mortgage on the property?
11. Is the mortgage assumable?
12. Will they take owner's terms?*
13. If they do not want owner's terms, but insist on cash, ask them what they are going to do with the cash. Perhaps their answer can help you. Maybe they are going to invest it to get a 9% return, often even 10%—that is, owner's terms!

Once you have found out what the seller really wants and needs (and never assume

---

Robert's Rule: Negotiating Price

Many people also make money by continually offering low prices for property they want to buy. That is, if someone is asking $40,000 and you think it is worth $35,000, many people will offer $10,000 or $15,000, just to see if people will take the bait. Of course, most people won't, but if you make enough of these offers, someone might accept one. You always want to offer as low a price as possible, because every dollar off the purchase price is a dollar that you save. Remember, you make money in real estate when you buy a piece of property.

Honest Profits

anything, you might be very surprised), ask for the following (some you'll get, some you won't):

1. Ask for owner's terms. If you get this, ask that no payments be due for one year, six months . . .
2. Ask to put nothing down.
3. If seller demands down payment, offer as little as possible.
4. Ask for a below market interest rate and long-term mortgage; i.e, 30-35 years.
5. Ask for the mortgage to be assumable and that it can be subordinated.
6. If owner financing is available, attempt to avoid personal liability on mortgages and notes. It's possible, but unlikely they'll agree to this—but you might as well ask.
7. If it is a rental property, ask for the rent to be included in your purchase price, so that you get credit for the next two or three months before the closing. That is, you get credited with three months' rent, while it remains the seller's duty to collect all rent.
8. Require that everything stay with the property—carpet, drapes, window treatments, appliances, air-conditioners, etc.
9. Tell the seller you would like to close as late as possible. The reason: If you are going to resell ("flip") the property, it gives you more than enough time to find another buyer; it also allows you time to think about the purchase, inspect the house, do thorough title searches, etc.
10. Ask the seller to pay all the closing costs and the cost of title insurance.
11. Ask the seller to provide a termite letter—that is, a letter guaranteeing that there is no termite damage. And, of course, if there is termite damage the seller should pay for correcting it.
12. Ask the seller to pay for repairs and/or upgrades, or at least give you credit off the purchase price for those repairs.

Real Life Example:

Recently I found a newspaper ad listing eight houses for sale which said "Owner financing possible, call." I immediately called the seller and I asked a lot of questions: where the properties are, how much they are renting for, what kind of financing was being offered. It was a very mixed bag of properties, but they seemed to be very good deals. The seller was offering: 20% down, a note for 20 years at 8% interest. I went and looked at the eight houses, which averaged about $31,000 apiece. Included were two duplexes, some single family homes, and two homes with a rather large tract of land. All of the homes were in pretty good shape, they were all rented, and the properties were properly cash flowing. Obviously, this seemed to be a very good deal.

I met the seller for lunch and spent quite a bit of time talking to him, asking my

Controlling, Holding, and Protecting Real Estate

1,000 questions. In my mind, I was very happy to offer the price that he was asking; and he told me (and I knew it was true) that there were many other people interested in this property. He felt very comfortable with me and my ability to actually close on the properties and manage them so he wouldn't have to take them back (this is a fear of all sellers who are taking owner's terms).

After asking a lot of questions, it finally became apparent *why* he was selling the properties. He was selling because he had inherited them through an estate settlement. He did not enjoy managing properties, he was not making money at it, he was not good at it, he had another job that took up a lot of time, and he didn't want to spend his time worrying about the properties. The main reason he wanted to sell the property was that there was some debt on the property that equaled about $50,000, and there was a note on the property that had $1088 due every month. When I uncovered this information, I offered him exactly what he wanted—to take over the note and give him the exact amount of money that he wanted just so he could pay off the debt. The end result: I got the property at a much lower price than I had originally anticipated (about $18,000 a house instead of $51,000) just by finding out what the seller needed. He was not interested in making money, and I was able to make sure he didn't! It actually cost him money to sell the property. He got what he wanted and I got a much better deal by asking questions.

"Weasel" Clauses: The Absolute Key to Reducing Your Risk.

The most important part of a contract, and one of the best kept secrets that you will learn, is drafting a "**Weasel**" clause. The weasel clause is what lets you sleep at night; it is what protects you during the controlling period. Basically, it is the simplest method to legally back out of a contract should you decide not to go through with the purchase of a property.

After you negotiate the best price and the best terms possible, you *absolutely must insert* the following language into the contract:

"**This contract is contingent upon** (choose one, a couple, or all of the following):

1. Buyer's inspection and approval of condition of property (3 days, 5 days, 30 days) before closing.

2. Buyer obtaining favorable financing.

3. Buyer's inspection and approval of utilities (5 days, 30 days) before closing.

4. Buyer's partner, spouse, uncle (whoever) approval.

5. Buyer's contractor approval.

6. Buyer obtaining a home inspection report agreeable to buyer.

7. Anything you can think of, if the seller allows you to insert it into the contract.

> ## Robert's Rule:
>
> Keep in mind that, if you have a motivated seller, you will be able to get all the weasel clauses you want.

Weasel clauses give you a way to back out of any purchase agreement. Essentially, they offer you a **risk-free** way to buy properties.

> ## Robert's Rule:
>
> *Never, ever* enter into a contract for the purchase of real estate without a weasel clause. I don't do it; neither should you. If a seller will not let you put it into a contract, walk away—unless the deal is an absolute steal and you are 100% sure that you can and will buy it.

You may put in other contingencies, such as contingent upon obtaining favorable financing, contingent upon your contractor coming in and giving favorable bids to do the repairs if it's a fixer-upper, contingent upon buyer's contractor inspecting and approving of the property, contingent upon buyer's inspection and approval of all utilities, paperwork, leases, tenant histories, inspection of completed title work, etc. **Keep in mind,** if you don't have a weasel clause then you are bound by the contract and must always close.

I highly recommend that you never put a contract on a property that you don't fully intend to close upon; but (**just in case**) you should always insert a weasel clause to give you a way out. If it seems like it may be a good deal, lock it up, put your weasel clause on the contract, then do your due diligence—and research, research, research the property.

Professional Secret.

Sometimes sellers are not the most ethical people. They may sign a contract with you and then try to sell the property to someone else, leaving you out in the cold. **Yes, this has happened, even to me (ONCE!).** There is a way for you to protect yourself once you sign a contract, but you must check it out with your local recording office (the office where documents regarding real estate are recorded). I would recommend that if you find a good deal, have a contract signed on it, then **go down to the recording office and file what is called an affidavit stating that you have a contract on the property, specifying the property address, the sellers' names, your name, and the purchase price. That way, if the sellers should be unethical and attempt to sell the property to someone else, they cannot pass title on that property because there is public notice that you have a contract on that property.** (By the way, an affidavit is really just a letter.)

Oftentimes, the recording office will ask for a copy of the contract to be recorded; sometimes you may be charged a fee or transfer fee, or a tax for recording the affidavit. By filing this, it will make it very difficult, if not impossible, for the sellers to pass title or sell the property to someone else. It will also be very difficult or almost impossible for another potential buyer to get title insurance on that property if you have recorded your affidavit (or contract). A title insurance company would look up the property and would find a copy of your contract or your affidavit stating that you have a contract on the property and would not insure the title to the new purchasers. In the event that sellers attempt to sell the property after entering into a contract with you (and you have not recorded anything), you can always go to court and sue them.

Suing people is a messy business—you're always better off making it a habit to record all of your deals. When I first got started, I learned my lesson very quickly. I signed a contract with a sellers, and the sellers sold the property to another party—which was both unethical and illegal. I immediately raced down to the courthouse upon hearing of this sale, and filed an affidavit at my local recording office. I then called the new purchaser of the property and the sellers and told them that they could not do this to me. They laughed at me said, "Oh, yes, we can," and that the property was being sold and there was nothing I could do about it. I then informed them that I had an affidavit and the contract filed at the courthouse before they had recorded their documents; therefore they could never get title insurance or ever really pass clear title to the property. They quickly quit laughing and began negotiating with me. I told them that I wanted all of my money that I was going to make on the sale of my contract in order for me to release my affidavit down at the courthouse. I was now in control and negotiated a very fair settlement with them. It wasn't until their check to me was cashed that I released my claim on the property. You must always be concerned with protecting yourself; filing an affidavit and a copy of the contract at the courthouse is one good way to insure you are protected.

Attorney's Note: Contracts.

Real estate contracts fall under the general law of contracts. Whether you have a two-sentence contract, a one-page contract, or a hundred-page contract, you are still subject to a certain amount of trust. Whether you sign a one-page contract or a five-hundred-page contract, if you are a liar, a cheater, and commit fraud, the length or intricacies of my contracts will not stop you from committing these acts. Therefore, it is very important for you to understand who you are dealing with before you sign a contract. I will teach you many intricacies that will protect you against many of these acts; but it is still important for you to know with whom you are dealing and if that person can be trusted. Unfortunately, in this day and age, I work under the premise that hardly anyone can be trusted; so I do everything in a contract to protect myself, which you also will learn how to do.

How to Take Title to a Property.

When you write a contract, one of the things you will have to put in (besides your very low purchase price and your favorable terms) is how you are going to take title to the property. This is a very often overlooked, yet fundamentally important question. How you take title to a property can greatly affect your liability and the transferability of the contract. It also may have grave implications for taxation down the road.

Personally, whenever I sign a contract or enter into a contract for the sale of real estate, I always insert "**Robert Shemin or assigns.**" In almost all states, contracts of almost any sort are assignable. That is, if you have a contract for the purchase of a house or the purchase of a truckload of beans (or almost anything) you can transfer *the right to buy it* to someone else. Therefore, to assure your right of assignability, you should put your name or "assigns" on each contract. That will definitely give you the right to assign the contract.

Should you have uneasy sellers who ask why you are putting "or assigns" in the contract, you can tell them that you may want to transfer the contract to another legal entity such as a trust, corporation, or partnership, or just another named party for the purpose of protecting your liability, which is true. You can also tell them not to worry, since all real estate contracts are assignable anyway (check your state law). **In all likelihood, these answers will make them feel more comfortable.**

Controlling, Holding, and Protecting Real Estate

The Various Ways to Title Real Estate.

When you buy real estate you are basically going into business. The first and most important question you need to ask yourself when you start a business is, "What form will this business take?" Normally, when you open up a small business (which you hope will grow into a large and profitable business), you have four alternatives: 1) A **sole proprietorship,** meaning the business and everything associated with it is in your name; 2) a **corporation,** whether a C-Corporation or a smaller type S-Corporation (meaning that the taxation is treated more like a partnership and the tax benefits and liabilities flow directly to you); 3) a **partnership**, if you are going into business with someone else; and 4) what in many states is known as a "**limited liability company**" (which can be great for running a real estate business).

When you go into a real estate business you have two additional options available: 1) You can take the real estate in the name of a trust; and 2) you can also form a **limited partnership** (which you will learn about later).

Some of my attorney friends make a living just consulting about and providing documentation about **trusts**. Most people have heard the word trust, but very few people understand exactly what a trust is. There are many different types of trusts, including living trusts (which are sometimes used instead of wills), revocable trusts (which can be changed at any time), and irrevocable trusts (which cannot be changed). There is also a special type of trust for real estate, commonly referred to as a **Land Trust.**

The general principle of a trust is simple: By creating a trust you are entrusting another person (or other legal entity) with an asset or piece of property. The person who manages the trust is called the **trustee** and probably has the highest legal duty known in law. That high legal duty is to the beneficiary of the trust, who could be yourself, your children, or whoever receives the benefits of what the trust owns. The trustee's duty is a **fiduciary** one; that is, the trustee must do whatever is in the beneficiaries' best interest. The trustee must do what the trust tells them to do and also must do what is in the best interest of the beneficiaries of that trust.

What is the real benefit to you of using a land trust? The main benefit is that the real estate is not in your name. More than likely, right now, I could go to the office where documents regarding real estate are recorded and look up your property address and find your name and/or your spouse's name. I could also easily call the property tax assessor's office and obtain the same information over the phone. Most states now have computerized systems so that, in a matter of seconds, I can discover all of the property that you own in any given county.

I cannot think of one benefit of having property in your name— unless, of course, you want to impress someone with how much property you own.

Honest Profits

Who is most likely to go look to see how property is titled or to see what assets are in your name? Unfortunately, the most likely candidates are attorneys who are attempting to suing you. If parties are suing you, they are going to find out who you are and what you own. An attorney can go down to the courthouse and punch up your name and find all the property you own. If you have substantial assets or own some real estate, it will show that you are a great person to sue because you have funds.

A land trust sets up a road block. When a property is taken in the name of a land trust, it is no longer in your name; it is now in the name of the trust. You can give whatever name you want to the trust. Personally, if I am buying 100 Apple Street, I call it the 100 Apple Street Trust. I have a separate trust for each property. Therefore, if I own a lot of property, and someone goes down to the courthouse and looks up addresses, all that will be found are the names of the trusts and the names of the trustees. You can name any persons as trustees, as long as they are legal, competent adults— friends, relatives, accountants, or attorneys.

If people try to find the owner of 100 Apple Street, they will find the 100 Apple Street Trust, Joe Smith, trustee. This creates a significant road block for the person trying to find out who owns the property. The next logical step is for the researcher to call the trustee. But when that person calls the trustee and asks, "Hey, Mr. or Mrs. Trustee, who owns 100 Apple Street (or who is the beneficiary of this trust)?" the trustee will be instructed to say, "I am sorry, as trustee I cannot tell you." A good lawyer will then ask, "Where can I find a copy of the trust so I can look up and see who the beneficiary is?" The trustee's response is simple: "Well, it is locked in my safe and I am not permitted to show it to you."

So the only way for someone to find out who owns the property is by having a court order the trustee to divulge the trust or reveal the name of the beneficiary. A major hassle, to say the least. Let's assume another scenario: Suppose a lawyer discovers (by word of mouth) that you are the owner of a certain piece of property upon which his/her lawyer believes a claim can be made. If you are dragged into court and asked (on the witness stand), "Do you own any property?" you can legally answer, No. Why? Because the trust owns the property; you are only the beneficiary of the trust. A smart lawyer will ask, however, "Are you the beneficiary of any assets or do you have a beneficial interest in any property?" Then, of course, you must answer yes. But how many "smart" lawyers are out there?

In the event that you are sued, land trusts put up a nice wall—certainly not a 100% unbreakable wall, but a nice wall that most litigants will have trouble knocking down. You may not think that this is important right now; but, unfortunately, frivolous lawsuits and litigation abound.

Another nice feature of land trusts is that they provide you with anonymity when you buy and sell properties. No one has to know that it is really you buying or selling a property, because it is in the name of a trust. Oftentimes I have sold property to friends and I did not want them to know that I was the seller. Luckily, I didn't have to reveal this because the property was held in the name of a trust. The trustee signed all the documents, received all the notices on the property, and handled all matters concerning the property for me. My name was never mentioned. Anonymity can be a great benefit when you are both *buying* and *selling* real estate.

There are disadvantages to a trust, too. The main one is more paperwork, and having to find someone else (the trustee), to handle all transactions regarding the real estate. This may cost you some money. These are minor nuisances, but it is important that you are aware of them.

There are no income tax implications for having property titled in the name of a land trust. As a matter of fact, some states do not recognize a land trust; but you can still put the property in the name of a trust and have the trustee listed as the contact person in matters concerning that property. It really does not affect the way you file your tax returns, except that you may have to list that the property is held in a trust.

The other main disadvantage to having property titled in a trust relates to borrowing money. Sometimes it confuses the lenders. Lenders will still want you to personally guarantee the property, because the property is not really in your name. Many people and banks believe that once you transfer property you own into a trust, it will trigger your **due on sale clause** in your mortgage. This belief is wrong; by law (federal banking law), a transfer of a property into a trust does not trigger the due on sale clause. The bank may be confused by this, but legally you are able to do this without a problem. Nevertheless, it may be a point of confusion for lenders and could cause borrowing delays from unsophisticated lenders.

Real Life Story.

Many large companies like Wal-Mart, K-Mart, or giant real estate purchaser buy real estate in the name of a trust. When they come into a small town, they do not want to advertise the fact that XYZ large, rich Fortune 500 company is buying property. They often do it in the name of a trust so that people will not suspect who is actually buying and therefore driving the cost of the land incredibly high.

Also, a few years ago, there was a case in Atlanta, Georgia, where a real estate developer was in big trouble with many banks. Some of his real estate was held in trust. The banks who were suing him hired some of the best attorneys in Atlanta to go after this gentleman. At one of the depositions they asked him, "Do you own any other real estate?" The real estate developer said, "No." They also asked, "Do you own any other property or assets?" and he said, "No." The developer was discharged from the

Honest Profits

case after a period of time; and since he had his real estate in the name of a trust, he was able to keep many millions of dollars' worth of real estate. Had they asked the question, "Are you the beneficial owner of any interests in real estate," or "Do you have any other interest in real estate?" he would have had to say, "Yes." The banks would have gotten back most or all of that property.

Are land trusts a foolproof, 100% protection against lawsuits and creditors? Absolutely not. But should you be sued or have people coming after you and trying to find out what you own, it will take them a lot longer to find out what you own if it is in the name of a trust—and it may offer you quite a bit of protection.

It is important to keep in mind that, if you transfer a property you personally own into the trust, after it has already been in your name, it can be traced back to you (just by looking to see who the transferee was) but again it will be difficult. Remember, just like anyone else, some attorneys are lazy. Sometimes they'll just call up the tax assessor's office or take a quick trip down to where deeds are recorded, and see what comes up in your name. Quite often, they will not do the tedious research to find out that you once owned other property. Again, once you transfer it into a trust, it will not be in your name.

HOW TO HOLD PROPERTY.
1. Your name (or your spouse's name).
2. Land trust.
3. Limited partnership.
4. General partnership.
5. Corporation: C-Corporation, S-Corporation, or Limited Liability Corporation.

Three issues to consider when deciding how to hold your property:
1) Taxes.
2) Liability.
3) Estate taxes and estate planning.

Let's examine all the various ways to hold property:
In your name, or you and your spouse's name.

Advantages: It is simple. Banks like it. Taxes are simple. Property is easy to transfer. You can put it in your will.

Disadvantages: You are an easy lawsuit target. Your name is on all public records. Should you be sued, for anything, the assets in your name can and will be easily attached. You will have insurance to cover these things, but no anonymity.

Controlling, Holding, and Protecting Real Estate

How Lawyers Work.

If you ever get sued for a car wreck that is your fault, an accident on your property, or as a result of your job, attorneys will sue you. First, if they have a claim and win, they will try to collect from your insurance company—if you have the *proper* insurance. Then, if the insurance is not enough, of if you do not have insurance, the attorneys will come after your assets—whatever they can find: your salary from work, home, cars, bank accounts. Obviously, if your assets are *titled in your name*, they will be easy to find. If you suddenly transfer them out of your name to your spouse's name, or that of a relative, or even a trust—it may be too late because the court may say you tried to hide your assets or you conveyed them fraudulently. If you are at risk of lawsuits, cannot get good insurance, and have assets, you may want to title your properties to a trust to protect yourself.

Land Trust.

Advantages: Property is not in your name. Difficult to find out the owner of the property. Many big companies use this to buy and sell property. Trustee does not have to tell anyone who owns the property unless a court orders it revealed. Anonymity—if you sell or "flip" the property, no one has to know you are involved or are making money. Should you be sued, it will take the attorney a long time to find out you own the property. The attorney may never find out.

Disadvantages: Trustee has to sign all documents. You must trust the trustee. Banks get a little confused. No tax or estate difference. Second, aggressive lawyers can break through the trust; but it is more work for them and you.

Limited partnership.

Advantages: Great asset protection, *except for the general partner*, who should be a corporation, and will be held liable. Good estate planning tool, as limited partnership interests can get a discount—because they are not easily marketed as real estate owned outright.

Disadvantages: General partner is liable, and some complex tax compliance issues. There are costs involved in setting these up, and paperwork to comply with the tax laws.

General Partnership.

Advantages: Simple to set up. Allows you to partner deals immediately.

Disadvantages: All partners are generally liable for the actions of the other partners. Generally, this is not a good way to own real estate.

Limited Liability Company.

Advantages: Probably the best way to own real estate. Liability protections, flexible tax advantages. Available in almost all states now.

Disadvantages: It is very new. Most states have enacted LLC statutes only recently. The IRS or some creative lawyers may find loopholes to attach liability to you.

Corporations.

Advantages: Property is not in your name. With an S-Corporation, tax advantages such as depreciation pass directly to owner. A big protection from personal liability. Giving away and selling property are easy. Corporations serve as another layer of protection from liability.

Disadvantages: Cumbersome taxes and paperwork. Banks will loan money to corporations, but most times require a personal guarantee. All corporation paperwork must be done properly. Must separately insure corporation. Corporate veil can be "pierced" to get to you.

If you are going to be a landlord, you'll want to set up a property management corporation. The job of the property management company is to collect all rents, pay all bills, hire help, manage property, and procure insurance. Generally, the corporation charges the owners of the property a commission, anywhere from 8-25% of the gross rent. If your property management company is managing properties that you own, 10% is a good commission. This commission pays your salary—and with a corporation, you must take a salary. Remember, owning property and managing it are two different things.

When you set up a property management company, tenants will not know that you are the owner of the corporation or the owner of the properties. You can be the good guy, working for a mean owner. Tenants do not call you at home, because they do not know who the owner of the property is.

A corporation is another layer of protection for you. It also makes you treat your business like a business—you work more regular hours, and it is separated from your personal life.

Summary.

Use land trusts to title most, if not all, of your properties. When filling out a contract, keep things out of your name. If you plan to buy a lot of real estate, you probably want to contact local counsel about forming a limited liability company if it is available in your state. S-Corporations and limited partnerships can also be very beneficial for purchasing and holding real estate.

If you plan to become a landlord, you will want to either set up or use a property management company, set up as a "limited liability company, or an S-Corporation to shield yourself from liability. Sign all documents in the corporation name, use your title, i.e., President; follow all incorporation procedures; be adequately insured; and maintain proper records and meetings. Many people set up corporations, but do not keep adequate records and files—which can nullify a corporation.

Please look into forming a limited liability company (LLC). Most attorneys and accountants seem to agree that it is probably the best way to own real estate. Again, unless you are in a high liability area and/or you own a lot of real estate, putting your real estate into a simple trust (to get your name off the public records) and making sure you are adequately insured will probably be enough to protect you.

INSURANCE: PROTECTING YOURSELF.

Make sure that any property you have title to is properly insured. Sometimes investment property can be added to your current homeowner's policy. Get an umbrella policy if possible.

Meet with your insurance agent annually to see if you are adequately insured. Shop around for the best policies and prices. Once you get more than a few policies you may be able to put them all under one policy, commonly referred to as a blanket policy.

If you are buying and rehabbing vacant property, it is often difficult and expensive to insure. Shop around, but make sure you are insured for the *full replacement value* of the property. If you are going to hold on to property for many years, make sure your policy adjusts for inflation or review your policies annually. If you don't, you could be underinsured in a few years. For rental property, you can insure appliances for just a few dollars extra a year; of course, if your deductible is high, it does not pay to insure them. Remember, anything attached to the property, i.e., central heating and air, or hot water heaters, are usually insured under your general policy.

Warning:

Whenever you use people to work on your properties, make sure they are subcontractors, not employees. You are liable for actions of employees. Have workers sign subcontractor agreements and check with local counsel. Generally, your regular insurance will not cover workers hurt on your jobs. If they are subcontractors, they

Honest Profits

should be responsible for their own actions, injuries, and insurance.

If workers are hurt and they are not insured, courts will typically find you liable. The best protection is to make sure that they are subcontractors. Each state varies, but some general rules about people working on your properties are to make sure that:

1. They use their own tools.
2. They either work for others (and not you), set their own hours, do not clock in, or they are their own bosses.
3. They have their own transportation and insurance and their own policies and procedures (for employees).
4. They carry their own workman's compensation insurance. **Get proof of insurance from them.**

In the event that people working on my properties do not have workman's compensation, I deduct the premium out of their pay and buy it for them. The cost is based on dollars earned and type of work. It is the only way to avoid costly liability in the event that an otherwise uninsured worker gets hurt on one of your properties.

Probably the best protection you can get, and the simplest, is proper, adequate insurance. Blanket policies of $1,000,000 or more of protection are usually only $500—1,000 a year above your normal policies. Assess your risks, the types of judgments assessed in your state, and how much and what type of insurance you have. If you have a lot of risk and a lot of assets, you probably need a lot of insurance. Buying extra insurance may be more effective and much simpler than forming and maintaining complex corporations or partnerships.

Overinsure yourself. Talk to your attorney and insurance agent about all of these liabilities and PROTECT YOURSELF!

CHAPTER 5

Turning Properties into Profit$

1. *Short-Term Profits.*

If You Have Little or No cash:

You want to buy property with as little (or no) cash out of your own pocket. Here are some ways to do this. You can try to assume the loan. You can ask the seller for **owner's terms**. You can even try to partner the deal with the seller—offer to fix up the property and sell it for a share of the profits (over and above a fixed price). If you have to borrow the money, try getting the money from friends and offer them a first mortgage and a higher rate of return than they can get on their money elsewhere. You can also try to partner a deal with a contractor or handymen. They do the work and you split the profits. Or you can partner a deal with a friend or a relative. The conversation will go something like this:

"Mary, I found a property that I could buy for $20,000. I'll spend $5,000 fixing it up, and then sell it for $45,000. What I need from you is a loan to buy the property, which will be secured by a first mortgage. I'll oversee everything and we'll split the profits. The work should be completed within 45 to 60 days and I should be able to sell the property within two to three months after that for $45,000. That's a $20,000 gain, of which you will receive $10,000. That's a 50% return on your money in less than five months."

I think you'll find Mary to be very interested. But, make sure your estimates are as close to accurate as possible. And you can be sure that if your first deal with your friend/relative goes well, that person will be more than happy to help you again. Make sure it is a good deal. Be professional. Analyze each deal and write it up. Put in contingencies, and be conservative.

If You Have Money.

If you have money, you need to determine what type of return you want in relation to your risk tolerance. When you are presented with a good deal on a home, you basically have three choices. Should you 1) flip it; 2) rehab and sell it; or 3) hold it

Honest Profits

for rental income and build wealth over time?
1) *Buy and Flip.*

> ## *Robert's Rule:*
>
> When flipping to other investors, don't be greedy. If you know you've found a great deal, sell it quickly for a medium/high profit. The likelihood of you selling the home to another investor for a big payoff is small and it's more likely you'll get the reputation of one who tries to overprice deals. That's not a reputation you want, because nobody will want to do business with you. The key is volume and medium profits. You cannot look at the flipping business as a one-time shot. When you sell a home to other investors, you want them to make a profit too. And you want to make sure they are happy with the deal. The key is to make friends in the business by letting others profit as well.

"Flipping a house" is a process whereby you **"lock up"** a house (that you know is a great deal), by putting a contract down on the house (obviously, the contract contains a right of assignment). You then sell the house to another investor/buyer (actually, you are really assigning the contract) for more money. If you decide to flip a home, this is where your network list becomes important. If you found a good deal, there's no doubt that there's another investor who is willing to buy the house from you for the right price.

Now is the time when your network list will come in handy. Once you have found your great deal and you want to flip the property, start calling potential buyers you know and offer them a deal on the home over and above the purchase price you offered. I have made anywhere from $2,000—$15,000 on a deal. Knowing what price to sell at depends upon your knowledge of what the market will bear. Factors such as the retail price of other homes in the area, how much work needs to be done on the house, and what investors typically pay for houses in the area, will aid you in your decision. And write up each deal with a picture, address, and analysis sheet.

The Anatomy of a Flip.

If you find a 1994 Mercedes convertible sports coupe in good condition that you can buy for $18,000 (a new one sells for $75,000+), do you think that you could sell

Turning Properties into Profit$

it and make some money? I hope your answer was yes.

If you find a house, duplex, or piece of land (or anything for that matter) worth $50,000 that you can buy for $25,000—OR—if it's worth $200,000 and you can buy it for $100,000—do you think that you can make money? As with the Mercedes, I hope your answer was yes!

One quick way to make money is to "flip it." Basically, it's buying and selling without putting any money down. Anytime you meet people who call themselves a "middlemen," this is exactly what they are doing. They are putting a buyer and seller together.

Here is how you can do it. Assuming you have read and learned everything I have written up to this point and have a very good handle on home values in your neighborhood, find a home that you know is undervalued whose *seller is motivated*. Suppose you know that the house should be valued at $80,000, but the seller is selling it for $60,000. You negotiate the seller down to $50,000 cash. You have two options:

1) Contract to buy the home for $50,000 to close in 45 days. Make sure both you and the seller sign. *Make sure you follow my rules for contracting (get your weasel clauses in there).* OR

2) Sign a 45-day option to buy the property for $50,000 cash. Make sure both you and the seller sign.

Okay. You now control the property *(make sure you record the contract or the option to protect yourself)*. But you have little or no cash and could never come up with $50,000 (or you can, but you're more interested in quick cash). So, what do you do? Find a buyer—quickly! Advertise this property to your **investor network list**, realtors, etc. Tell everyone that the house is worth $80,000 but that they can buy it for $65,000, but must do so within 30 days.

Okay. You've found your buyer. Now:

1) You assign your contract (almost every contract is assignable unless it specifically states otherwise) for $15,000 (the difference between your purchase price and the price you are selling it for). By assigning it, you're basically allowing the new buyer to step into your shoes. So the new buyer will purchase the house from the original seller for $50,000, and the new buyer pays me $15,000 for the right to purchase the house for $50,000. You make $15,000.

2) Sell your option to buy the house for $15,000. The new buyer executes the option and closes on the house for $50,000. You make $15,000.

3) You sign a contract with the new buyer to sell the house for $65,000. At the closing, you have what is known as a **collapsed closing**. Your buyer comes in at 2:00 p. m. and gives the closing attorneys (or title company) $65,000 to buy the property. At 2:30 p. m., the original seller comes in, signs the deed, and collects a check for

75

Honest Profits

$50,000. You get a check for $15,000. The title passes from the original seller to the ultimate buyer. It sounds fantastic. It happens every day. Some deals make you $500, $1,000, $5,000, $15,000. And some people flip large deals, apartment buildings, land, office buildings, and make tens of thousands of dollars. Try it, and you'll like it.

NOTE! Some states have fraud laws that prohibit this type of transaction because you signed a contract to sell a piece of property that you do not have title to and had to use someone else's money to obtain that title. Of course, if you disclose what you are doing, in writing, to the ultimate purchaser, it is probably not fraud. Make sure you check with your attorney on this. Nevertheless, assigning contracts and selling options is always preferable. See Disclosure Form in Appendix.

Advantages: Good, quick money. You do not need capital to begin.

Disadvantages: You must know buyers who have the money to purchase quickly. If you are not able to close on the properties you lock up, word will get around not to do business with you. In addition, sometimes people will get upset when they learn that you were a middle-person and that you made a lot of money. Buyers and sellers may try to walk away from the deal. Also, on flips, rehabbing, and reselling, the IRS will consider you a dealer. These activities will be listed as a separate type of business and you will be taxed on your profits about 15% beyond your regular tax rate. This is called a type of self-employment tax. Of course, you hardly ever pay taxes unless you make money.

2. Medium-Term Profits.

Buy, Rehab, and Sell.

Suppose you don't like flipping or you don't think you can make much money on the home in its present condition. Still, you know that with an inexpensive face lift, the house will sell for a lot more than you bought it for. The key to rehabbing a property is a good, reliable, and inexpensive contractor; or better yet, you do the work yourself. Just as important is that you never underestimate:

Holding costs—mortgage payments, taxes, insurance, utilities, etc. ; 2) The price you think you can sell the property for, once you fix it up (be conservative—if I think the house will sell for $70,000, I discount it by 15% ($59,500) to determine whether I will profit from the sale of the home. Anything above $59,500 is pure gravy. It is always better to make more money than you thought than it is to make less.

Your goal: To get the precise information you need from contractors and others who will allow you to establish the actual value to fix up the home so you can buy it for at least 40% off retail and sell it profitably in today's market.

Here's something else to remember when you are thinking of what it will take to fix up a property and sell it. A UCLA communications researcher states the following:

- Your verbal message accounts for 7% of what is believed.
- Your vocal message accounts for 38% of what is believed
- Your visual message accounts for 55% of what is believed.

That's why you need to dress up your properties, providing ceiling fans and the like. Hiring landscapers can give your property a high perceived value.

One more valuable tip: If you're short of cash on a particular deal and you believe it's necessary to get the landscape in better shape in order to get top dollar, here's a clever way to get the job done using none of your own hard-earned money. Approach a landscaper and say, "Look, if you do the landscaping on this job and you'll wait two months (or whatever time it takes) for your money until I sell the home, I'll pay you double your ordinary fee." If you can get one landscaper to go for this deal, you can save a great deal of money. You can also try this gambit with appliance, carpeting, paint, plumbing, drape and other individual contractors as well.

Robert's Rule of Rehab:

Once you have triple-checked your projected expenses and have determined that you will net less than a 40% return, you should *not* attempt the rehab project. Why so conservative? There are too many things that can go wrong.

For example: Suppose you buy a house for $32,000. Estimated repair expenses are $12,000, and holding costs are estimated at $3,500, for a grand total of $47,500. You had better be able to sell the property for at least $66,500 (net) —a minimum 40% return. You'll need at least a 40% cushion of safety for the following reasons: If the contractor takes a much longer time getting the job done; if your property does not sell for a year; if your buyers cannot qualify for a loan, if there are unforeseen repairs, extra holding costs, etc.

Always keep in mind that more than 50% of rehab projects lose money. Don't be ruled by emotions; be ruled by logic and numbers.

Advantages: **There is great money to be made. You are creating housing and helping to uplift an area by fixing up a home. You can do some of the work yourself and save money. You don't have to deal with tenants.**

Disadvantages: **Ties up capital for months or possibly a year while you rehab and wait to sell. Contracting and rehabbing can be time-consuming and frustrating. Remember, you may also pay an extra 15% of your profits in** self-employment tax.

Lease Purchasing.

Lease purchasing is an excellent way to control real estate without using any (or much) of your own money. It is also an excellent option to keep in mind when you find a property that just isn't good enough for a flip, or one you want to buy and hold but for which you don't have the down payment.

Here's how a lease purchase works. You negotiate a long term lease with the seller for as low a monthly payment as possible and as low a deposit as possible. You also get a purchase price for which you can buy the property at any time before your option period expires (which should be as long as the lease). Make sure that the lease allows

---

Robert's Rule:

Are you tired of landlording headaches?

Frustrated by those stupid, bothersome repair calls?

Then, lease purchasing might be the answer to your prayers.

Instead of just renting, lease purchase the property and make the tenant responsible for all repairs.

In fact, you can start right now with the tenants you currently rent to.

Explain to them that you're going to help them buy their home.

Get as large a deposit from the lease purchaser as is possible.

You can use part of the rent they pay as an incentive toward a down payment—only if it's on time.

It's a great incentive for them and will probably cause them to pay their rent more consistently.

In fact, you can put into the agreement that if they don't pay their rent on time, they'll lose their deposit and their down payment savings.

Always use a separate lease and option agreement.

Why? A couple of reasons.

If you have to evict the person, you can go to court with the lease.

If the option is attached to a part of the lease, a judge may deem the agreement to be a purchase and not rule in your favor for a timely eviction.

Also, the deposit should be the money paid for the option to avoid having to pay it back to the renters in the event they decide not to buy the property.

for subletting.

You then turn around and rent or lease purchase the property to someone else for a higher monthly rent and a higher purchase price. You now earn money every month and can profit if your lease purchaser actually buys the property for the higher price.

Example: You negotiate with Joe Seller to lease purchase his house for a $200 deposit and $250 per month rent and a purchase price of $59,000, all of which is good for three years. Then, you turn around and lease purchase the property to Jill Buyer for a $1,000 deposit (option money or a security deposit), $450 per month rent and an option to buy the property for $65,000, all good for two years. Your profit potential is $800 up front ($1,000 security deposit minus your $200 security deposit). The $200 per month on the difference is the rental rate, and if Jill buys the home, you just made $6,000.

Lease purchasing is a hybrid form of investing—some landlording, some flipping. Here are some other lease purchasing ideas.

When you lease purhase, have part of your rent go towards paying down the purchase price. Example: If you pay $250 per month, have $50—$100 per month (or as much as you can negotiate) go toward reducing your purchase price.

You can also have the original seller be responsible for repairs just as if you were renting. However, when you lease purchase the property, make your lease purchaser be responsible for the first $200—$500 worth of repairs. Simply explain to purchasers that if it is going to be their house, they might as well start taking care of it.

How Do You Find Properties to Lease Purchase?

1. Look in your newspaper for "For Rent" ads. Call the landlord/owners and ask them if they would be interested in lease purchasing the property to you. Ask them how often they have had trouble collecting the rent. You can guarantee (because you are a nice, reputable person) that they will get their rent on time every month for 1, 2, 5, 10, 20 years. Try to get them to be responsible for the first $1,000 of repairs, but assure them that you will handle all repair problems. Most landlord/owners are tired of managing their properties. This is an excellent way to alleviate their problems.

2. Call property managers and guarantee them a certain rent every month. Have the manager help you negotiate with with the owner. The manager should be happy you will be paying the rent—even if it's less than market rent (having it paid at all is sometimes worth a lot). Also, negotiate so that the manager gets a commission if the property is sold. Remember, property managers get a commission every time the rent is paid. The manager will be getting paid and you will be doing a lot of their work. It's a great deal for the property manager.

3. See chapter on Locating Properties.

Honest Profits

Advantages of Lease Purchasing. You can develop a good monthly income with little headache (if you are able to negotiate away the repair responsibilities). If you can clear $200 a month on every lease purchase house, you can make yourself a nice steady income. How about 10, 20, or 30 houses, times $100 or $200 a month? Meanwhile, you are collecting larger deposits on option money from your lease purchaser, so you can make thousands of dollars up front. And don't forget the back end, when your tenant decides to purchase the house. It is a great way to control and profit in real estate without the risks of ownership and without tying up a lot of your money. Your option to buy is less than your purchaser's option price, so the difference is your profit.

3. Long-Term Profits.

If you found a great deal on a home, you may find that holding it and renting it out is the best strategy. It provides decent cash flow and allows your tenants to pay off your mortgage and builds your wealth over the long term. In addition, the income that you earn will probably be nearly nontaxable because of all the deductions and depreciation you are allowed; consult your accountant. Obviously, the downside is that you have to be a landlord, and that means dealing with tenants. If you don't like working with people, landlording is not for you. It requires patience, an ability to understand yet be tough, and the ability to manage a business. You must run the business. Do not let the business run you. Set up a system, policies, and procedures—and follow the system. Be professional, not emotional.

Introduction to Section 8.

Here are twelve powerful wealth-building reasons why you should concentrate your landlording efforts in the low-cost housing area.

Let the government pay all or most of your rent.

1. It's a niche everyone is avoiding or virtually ignoring.
2. There is little competition.
3. Rent is guaranteed for 12 months with Section 8. No bounced checks!
4. Tax consequences are excellent.
5. Cash flow can be controlled if you buy right.
6. Capital appreciation is excellent.
7. Diversification reduces risk.
8. Depreciation is a powerful factor.
9. Tax credits are available and can be held or sold for almost instant income.

10. Leveraging property into perpetuity is possible.

11. You can get some of the best deals in real estate in low- to moderate-income housing.

What is the Section 8 Program?

The Section 8 Program is a rental assistance program which assists eligible people by paying a portion of their rent to a private owner. The program is funded by the U. S. Department of Housing and Urban Development (HUD) and applied by your State Housing Development Agency (Human Resource Agency or City Housing Agency).

Who is eligible for assistance?

An applicant must be a member of a family (two or more persons related by blood, marriage, or with evidence of a stable family relationship) , or age 62 or older, or disabled, or handicapped if under age 62, or a single eligible person. The applicant must have gross annual income below the income limits set by the U. S. Department of Housing and Urban Development. The applicant cannot have an outstanding debt to a public housing agency.

Note: There is usually a waiting list for persons applying for assistance!

What types of properties qualify?

A family may choose an apartment, a duplex, a single family house, or a mobile home. The unit must be the correct size for the family. It may not be owner occupied. The unit must be in good condition and pass an inspection. The inspection determines compliance with HUD's Housing Quality Standards. A summary of Housing Quality Standards is found below.

How does an owner determine that a family is eligible for Section 8?

A family must be issued a certificate or voucher before they begin to look for a unit of housing. The certificate or voucher states that the family is eligible and shows the period of time they have to search for a housing unit, usually 60 days. If they cannot find an acceptable unit before the certificate or voucher expires, they lose it. The certificate or voucher is given to the next person on the waiting list.

Note: An owner should always contact the local staff before making any commitment to a family. The unit must pass inspection, and a lease and contract must be signed before the family moves into the unit and before subsidy payments may

Honest Profits

begin.

Most Section 8 certificate and voucher holders are single mothers, elderly, and/or handicapped people.

Is there much paperwork for an owner?

The owner must sign one lease with the tenant. The owner may use the state's HUD model lease or his or her own lease with a HUD addendum. (The owner may not have a tenant sign more than one lease.) The owner also signs a contract with the local HUD office. The contract authorizes the payments to the owner. The local staff prepares the lease and contract.

How much rent may an owner charge?

If the family holds a certificate, the amount of rent which may be charged is limited by the fair market rent for the particular county and bedroom size.

Fair market rents are set by HUD. The amount paid for rent to the owner, plus utilities, may not exceed the fair market rent.

Important: The family is not allowed to make up any difference in what an owner wants for rent and the amount allowed by the fair market rent. In addition, the rent the owner charges must also be comparable to similar unassisted units in the same neighborhood. And the owner may not charge more to rent a Section 8 unit than he or she would receive for renting the unit to a private, unassisted tenant.

If the family holds a voucher, there is no limit on the amount of rent an owner may charge a unit. There is, however, a limit on the amount of subsidy which will be paid on a tenant's behalf. The tenant is allowed to pay the difference between the rent and the subsidy. The agent may counsel a family concerning the advisability of renting a unit if the rent appears excessive. The agent may refuse to admit a unit to the program if the rent requested by the owner is not comparable to similar, nonassisted units in the neighborhood.

Does the tenant pay any of the rent?

Under the program, tenants pay according to their income.

If the family is a certificate holder, they pay no more than 30% of their monthly adjusted income.

If the family holds a voucher, they pay more than 30% if the rent and utilities exceed the payments standard.

Important: The amount the family pays may change during the year if the family's income or composition changes. An owner is notified in writing of any changes in the amount the tenant pays. It is the owner's responsibility to collect the tenant's portion of the rent. An owner may evict a tenant who does not pay his/her portion of the rent. Many tenants on Section 8 have all of their rent paid for by the government directly to you.

Who pays the utilities?

This arrangement is negotiated between the landlord and tenant and specified in the lease. Regardless of who pays which utilities, every unit must have electricity; an adequate, acceptable, permanent heat source; running water; hot water; a stove, and a refrigerator.

I recommend that the tenants pay their own utilities when possible. It is difficult to control utility usage. Of course, if the landlord pays, they are allowed more rent.

Who chooses the tenants?

Section 8 staff are responsible for determining if an applicant is eligible for subsidy. They do not screen applicants as potential tenants. Screening for desirable tenants is the responsibility of the owner. An owner does not have to accept tenants simply because they hold a certificate or voucher. You as a landlord should and must screen all tenants.

How often are inspections done?

An inspection must be done, and the unit must pass inspection before the tenant moves into the unit. If the tenant currently occupies the unit, it must pass the inspection before the tenant is admitted to the program. After the initial inspection, subsequent inspections are done every twelve months for as long as the unit remains on the program. Special inspections may be done if the owner or tenant requests it, or as part of an audit.

It is the owner's responsibility to make all repairs and to maintain the unit so it always passes housing quality standards. Rental payments may be abated for any period in which a unit does not pass housing quality standards.

If a tenant damages a unit or takes action which causes the unit not to pass housing quality standards, it is the owner's responsibility to make any needed repairs or corrections. The owner may bill and/or evict the tenant for tenant damages.

How long is the family eligible for assistance?

A family is certified as eligible for a twelve-month period. Their eligibility must be recertified every twelve months. This is called the anniversary date. If a family's eligibility has not been recertified before the anniversary date, the payments automatically stop at the end of the twelfth month. Payments are resumed as soon as eligibility is recertified.

A family may continue receiving assistance as long as they continue eligible, and the unit passes housing quality standards. If a family vacates a unit, the payment of that unit stops. The owner should always notify the agent if the family vacates.

If a family's assistance is terminated because of: their failure to cooperate, fraud, or their income being too high, the landlord is notified that assistance will stop. If the landlord agrees, the tenants may remain in the unit and pay all of the rent themselves.

May an owner evict a Section 8 tenant?

An owner may evict a tenant under the terms of the lease. The owner must follow state and local laws of eviction.

Are rental increases allowed?

An owner desiring a rental increase may request one every 12 months at the time of the contract anniversary date. If a unit is occupied by a certificate holder, the amount of the increase is controlled by adjustment factors published by HUD. In addition, the rental increase may be given only if the new rent will be comparable to that of other, nonassisted units in the same neighborhood.

If an owner desires a rental increase, he must make the request in writing to the agent at least 60 days prior to the contract anniver-sary date. The owner's request should include how much of an increase is desired and the reason(s) the increase is requested.

Reasons for rental increase may include the following:

(a) increased taxes, (b) increased utility bills, (c) property improvements.

Verification should be provided on the above. The agent will notify the owner of the amount of the increase.

The agent may refuse an increase if an owner has failed to maintain the property; if there appears to be no justification for an increase; or if comparable nonassisted units rent for less.

If the unit is occupied by a voucher holder, the owner determines the amount of the increase. The owner must notify the tenant and the agent of the increase at least 60 days prior to the contract anniversary date. The tenant decides whether or not to accept the increased rent. The subsidy may not change, so the tenant may have to pay the increase. If the tenant cannot pay the additional rent, the tenant may choose to relocate. The agent may advise the tenant on the appropriateness of the increase.

Does the tenant's portion of the rent ever change?

The amount that the tenant pays varies according to the family's income and number of members in the family. For voucher holders, it also depends upon the amount of the rent. If at any time the family or HUD's portions change, the owner will receive a written notice.

Rental assistance is based mainly on the tenants' income. If the tenants' income goes up, then they may be required to pay more of the rent. By the way, unpaid tenant rent may be collectible as damages.

Is an owner eligible to collect the rental subsidy payment once a tenant moves?

No. When a tenant vacates a unit or dies, the contract and lease become void. Any checks received after the tenant vacates should be returned.

What about unpaid tenant rent and tenant damages?

If tenants do not pay their portion of the rent, an owner should begin eviction proceedings. If a tenant damages a unit, the owner must make the repairs. The agent should be contacted prior to making the repairs. The owner should then bill the tenants for the repairs. If there are unpaid tenant damages and/or rent after tenants vacate a unit, the owner may apply for reimbursement for these items. How much is paid depends upon whether the tenant held a voucher or a certificate. For specific details, see the section on Procedures for Filing Claims, below.

When/how does an owner get his rental money each month?

The owner is responsible for collecting the tenant's portion of the rent. This should be collected on the first of the month. An owner may designate late charges. However, these late charges must be stated as an addendum to the lease.

The agency's portion of the rent is mailed on the first working day of each month for the following month. Any adjustment moneys or amounts owed for prior months are sent on special checks. The check will be automatically stopped at the end of the contract anniversary day if the renewal process has not been completed. Once the renewal is received and processed by the agency, the payments resume. The first check for a new tenant may take six to eight weeks since a file must be established in the state computer system. Once the file is established, checks may be issued.

How does an owner become a Section 8 landlord?

Contact the local Section 8 staff in your area for information.
It is probably administered by your state or city housing agency.

May an owner sell property occupied by a Section 8 tenant?

The sale should be coordinated with the local staff. The buyer must be willing to honor the Section 8 lease and contract. The seller should advise the buyer of the Section 8 obligation and turn over any security deposits held for the tenant.

What are the advantages of being a Section 8 landlord?

- A portion of the rent is guaranteed and comes in like clockwork every month. There are no bounced checks—which could be a real problem with some low-cost-housing tenants.
- There is some reimbursement for unpaid tenant rent.
- There is some reimbursement for damages.
- It's an area of housing that many real estate people are avoiding or ignoring.
- There is the potential for federal income tax credit.
- There is potential for excellent cash flow, capital appreciation, and depreciation.
- Distressed housing that can be rehabbed can dramatically increase your bottom line.

What are your responsibilities and obligations as a Section 8 landlord?

- Routine management functions such as screening and selecting tenants, maintaining the property, rent collection, and handling tenant problems. Participation in the programs does not relieve a landlord of any normal duties. The programs simply pay all or a portion of the tenants' rent.
- The landlord must comply with all the requirements contained in the lease and agency contract.
- To maintain the unit at all times so it always passes HUD's housing quality standards. (See Summary of Housing Quality Standards below.) Owners are responsible for repairs even if damages are tenant caused. The tenant may be charged for any damages which are tenant caused. Eviction may be considered for tenant damage.
- To collect only the amount of rent from the tenant which is specified in the

lease or agency contract or any interim adjustment notices. Any charges in addition to the monthly rent must be stated in the lease or lease addendum.
- To notify the local staff if a tenant is being evicted. State and local laws governing eviction must be observed.
- To notify the local representative immediately if the tenant vacates the unit. Landlords are not eligible to receive rental payments if the tenant is not living in the unit. The agency contract automatically terminates if the tenant leaves the unit. Any rental payments received following the month the tenant vacates the unit is to be returned to the agency.
- To notify the local staff and tenant at least 60 days prior to the lease anniversary date if a rental increase is requested for the next year.
- To comply with all HUD/agency requirements in order to be eligible to file claims for tenant damages, unpaid rent, or vacancy loss. See Procedures for Submitting Claims.
- To immediately report to the local staff if any utilities are disconnected, whether paid for by the tenant or landlord. If a tenant or landlord fails to fulfill the obligation to connect/pay utilities as outlined in the lease, rental subsidy will be abated and/or terminated.
- To provide proof of ownership of a unit.

To provide a W-9 for purposes of filing a correct 1099 with the IRS.

Failure to fulfill these obligations and requirements may result in the withholding, abatement, or termination of housing assistance payments. Future participation in the programs may be prohibited.

A Summary of Housing Quality Minimum Standards.

These standards may vary from area to area. Generally they require that a unit be safe, clean, and be up to codes/standards.

I like Section 8 as it makes me keep my units in top shape.

a. The unit must have a separate living area, kitchen, bathroom and a bedroom for each two persons.

b. The living room must have two electrical outlets in working condition. An overhead light may be considered as one outlet. The living room must have a window. If the window was designed to be opened, it must be operable.

c. The kitchen must have one electrical outlet and an overhead light in working condition. There must be a stove and refrigerator in good, workable condition. These two items maybe furnished by the tenant or landlord. There must be adequate space for storage and a sink with hot and cold running water. The sink cannot have leaks and must have a proper trap.

d. The bathroom must have a toilet, tub or shower, and a sink. All fixtures must be workable, without leaks, and with proper traps. The bathroom must have an exterior, operable window or a vent. There must be one permanently installed light fixture.

e. All bedrooms must have two workable electric outlets. An overhead light may be considered as one outlet. The bedroomsmust have an exterior window.

f. All electrical wiring must be safe. Cover plates must be on all outlets, and there must not be any frayed or exposed wiring.

g. All utilities must be connected by the landlord or the tenant. A unit without utilities is considered substandard.

h. There must be a permanent heat source in safe, operating condition. Unvented space heaters, kerosene heaters, and portable electric heaters should not be considered as the permanent heat source. The heat system must be capable of providing heat directly or indirectly to all rooms used for living.

i. Each unit must have a properly installed and operating hot water heater. The hot water heater must have a temperature and pressure sensitive relief valve. There must be a discharge line pointing toward the floor or drained to the exterior of the unit. Gas hot water heaters must be properly vented.

j. All operable windows must have locks. Windows must be unbroken, secure, and weather-tight.

k. All exterior doors must be secure, weather-tight, and lockable.

l. All glass in windows and doors must be unbroken and free of cracks.

m. All interior and exterior surfaces of the unit must be free of cracked, peeling paint.

n. All steps (interior and exterior) of four or more must have handrails, possibly on both sides.

o. All porches and balconies higher than 30" off the ground must have rails designed so a child may not crawl through and sturdy enough to support a person who might be falling.

p. All interior and exterior surfaces, including the walls, floors, ceilings, roofs, and foundations must be free of holes, cracks, leaks, and other deterioration which would pose a hazard or allow wind/rain into the unit.

q. The yard must be free of debris, garbage, trash, etc.

r. The unit must be free of bugs, mice, rats, and other vermin.

s. All mobile homes must have tie downs.

t. All units must have a fire alarm or smoke detector in working condition on each level.

u. The roof and gutters must be free of defects which allow air or water infiltration.

v. All entrances to crawl spaces should be covered, and exterior vents should be covered with screens.

w. The water and sewer system must be served by an approvable public or private system.

x. All plumbing must be free of leaks or corrosion and be properly vented.

y. All units must have private access without going through any other unit's living area. All units must have sufficient access and egress to provide an alternative means of escape in case of fire.

z. Each room used for sleeping or living which has one or more windows made to be opened must have a screen on at least one window, unless the unit has central air-conditioning.

Important note:

This is a summary list only. A more detailed explanation of housing quality standards is found in the HUD Handbooks for administering the Section 8 Programs.

No lease or contract should ever be signed until a unit meets housing quality standards.

It is the landlord's responsibility to maintain the unit so it always meets housing quality standards. If a tenant causes a unit to become substandard, the landlord must make the necessary repairs. The landlord may bill the tenant for the repairs or initiate eviction proceedings if appropriate. When a landlord endorses the housing assistance payment each month, he/she is certifying that the unit meets housing quality standards.

If HUD or their representatives determine that a unit is substandard and the landlord refuses to make the necessary repairs within a designated period of time, the housing assistance payment may be abated or canceled.

Procedures that must be observed for filing claims for unpaid tenant rent, damages, or vacancy loss.

- Know whether the tenant holds a certificate or voucher. A landlord may file for unpaid tenant rent, damages, and/or vacancy loss for tenants who hold certificates.

  Important: There is no provision for vacancy loss for tenants who hold vouchers.
- The maximum amount which may be paid to a landlord for claims against certificate holders is two months' contract rent minus the security deposit; for voucher holders, the maximum amount is one month's contract rent minus the security deposit.
- The amount of the security deposit which was collected or could have been

collected under the rules of the program will always be deducted from a claim. Therefore, it is always to the landlord's advantage to collect a security deposit. The Section 8 staff will inform the landlord of the maximum amount of security deposit which may be collected.
- Any claim must be submitted to the Section 8 staff within 60 days of the date the tenant vacates the unit. The agency reserves the right of refusal to pay any claims not submitted within the 60-day deadline.
- There are three types of claims.

FLASH! Damage claim rules are being changed. Check with your local HUD office.

1. Damage Claims (certificates and vouchers):

- Damage claims are to reimburse expenses incurred by a landlord for actual damages to a unit by a tenant family. This does not include theft of items from the unit or normal routine cleaning and replacement due to wear and tear.
- Items stolen from a unit should be reported to the local law enforcement agency. Landlords may want to carry insurance protection for stolen property.
- Damage claim provisions DO NOT cover regular maintenance, repair, and replacement which are routine functions due to normal wear and tear, or when rental units experience turnover of tenants.
- Damage claim provisions DO NOT cover damages to furniture or draperies. The contract rent amount under the Section 8 Program is for an unfurnished unit. The program assumes no responsibility for furniture or draperies.

Example #1. 1: Painting is routine maintenance expected in rental property. Painting should not be included in a damage claim except under extraordinary circumstances such as pictures/writing being done on the wall with spray paint, etc.

Example #1. 2: Routine carpet cleaning is a part of normal maintenance. Carpet cleaning/replacement should be included only if actual damage was done. For example, the tenants worked on their motorcycle in the living room. The carpet was torn and motor oil spilled on the carpet.

If a landlord believes he/she has actual damage to a unit when a tenant moves, this is what to do:

a) Contact the Section 8 staff so an inspection may be done. The staff must verify the damage to the unit. No repairs should be made until the inspection is completed.

b) The repairs must be completed and a copy of the receipts for the labor and supplies submitted with the claim. Estimates may not be used. The bills/receipts should indicate the purposes of the supplies and/or labor. For example: "Plumbing supplies to repair damage to bathroom."

claim.

d) The HUD form for filing claims must be signed and dated. This form is available from the staff. The HUD form must be accompanied by copies of the bill to the tenant and the receipts for the repairs.

e) The claim will be reviewed by the staff. Items not allowed will be deducted from the total claimed. The value of replacement items will also be considered. For example, if the carpet in a room has to be replaced due to damages, the full value of the replacement carpet would not be allowed unless the carpet which was damaged was new when the ten-ant moved into the unit. Depreciation will be taken into consideration.

f) Regardless of the extent of damage, there is a limit on the amount which may be reimbursed. The land-lord may continue efforts to obtain reimbursement from the tenant.

2. Unpaid Rent Claims (certificates and vouchers) :

- A landlord should not allow a tenant to accumulate a large unpaid rent debt. It is the landlord's responsibility to evict a tenant for nonpayment of rent. The landlord should not depend on the agency or the staff to collect rent.
- If a tenant vacates a unit owing unpaid rent, the landlord must first attempt to collect the rent from the tenant. Proof of this attempt must accompany the claim.
- The landlord must file an itemized statement with the claim showing the months and amounts of unpaid rent.
- Regardless of the amount of unpaid tenant rent, there is a limit on the amount which may be reimbursed. The landlord may continue efforts to collect from the tenant.

3. Vacancy Loss Claims (certificates only) :

- The landlord must immediately notify the Section 8 staff of a vacancy loss if the tenant moved in violation of the lease.
- The landlord must make every effort to rent the unit. Proof of this effort, such as copies of newspaper ads, must accompany a claim. Attempts to rent the unit may include making it available to other certificate or voucher holders who are looking.
- The landlord must notify the Section 8 staff of the date the unit is rented.
- The landlord must sign the HUD claim form which is furnished by the Section 8 staff

- If the landlord evicts a tenant, he/she may apply for vacancy loss only if he/she complied with the terms of the Agency contract and lease and all applicable laws.

Payment for vacancy will be made as follows:
- For the month the tenant vacated the unit, the owner will receive the housing assistance payment due under the contract for as much of the month as the unit remains vacant.
- If the unit remains vacant after the month the vacancy occurred, the landlord may claim a housing assistance payment in the amount of 80% of the contract rent for a vacancy period not to exceed one additional month, or the expiration of the lease, whichever comes first. Any amounts paid by the tenant, including any remaining security deposit, will be deducted from the payment to the landlord. If the unit is rented the month following the vacancy, the vacancy loss payment will be paid only for the vacant days.

Points to Remember:
- Contact the Section 8 staff immediately when a vacancy occurs.
- The HUD claims form must be signed.
- Documentation of the claim must be provided.
- The unit must be inspected if a damage claim is involved.
- The claim must be submitted within 60 days of the vacancy.

How to avoid the need for claims:
- Screen tenants carefully and only select solid, responsible tenants.
- Make regular inspections of each unit. (This is not the Section 8 staff's job!)
- Deal with tenant problems immediately. If a tenant is damaging a unit or not paying the tenant portion of the rent, take action quickly. Very quickly!

The keys that practically insure excellent results in the low-cost housing area:

There is little competition in several housing niches that I've discovered. Many landlords avoid these potentially lucrative niche markets because they hear a few publicized horror stories about tenant damage. I've found that if you screen your tenants properly, treat people decently, reward them for responsible behavior, and show them you are doing everything in your power to contribute to community service—and follow my rules precisely—you can actually reduce your repair expenses.

What's more, irresponsible landlords (many of your competitors) neglect their properties and their tenants and some even try to gouge tenants.

Quite honestly, 99% of my 140-plus tenants are downright decent people. Obviously there's a rotten apple in almost any real estate management operation. On the other hand, if you keep your property clean and follow my plan in selecting responsible tenants, this type of tenant will seek you out. This, in turn, will allow you to be even more selective within the framework of the rules. Sounds too easy, I know; yet many landlords with a different mindset overlook these profit-boosting techniques. They expect the worst tenants, and, of course, that's exactly what they attract.

How to Be the Best Landlord.

Every year a ton of businesses go belly up, leaving their owners wondering what went wrong. Meanwhile, a few small business people keep thriving, many of them delivering profits beyond their owners' most optimistic dreams.

What makes the difference? Well, it's certainly not luck, that's for sure. Quite simply, it's the management's ability to inspect their business and take care of their tenants on a timely basis.

How to interview prospective tenants over the phone.

1. Be very cheerful, positive, and polite. This may sound silly, but this first point will automatically put you in the top 2% of all landlords. Remember: You are selling your unit.

2. Get each person's name and phone number.

3. Ask the people what they are interested in.

4. See if you can meet their needs. If not, tell them to pass the word around about what you have available, or ask them to call back if you think you may have something for them later. Tell them all of the positive aspects of your unit. Details are important, i. e., carpet, mini-blinds, washer-dryer hookups, ceiling fans, type of yard, location.

5. Never reveal to parties ahead how much the rent is. Always ask them, "How much are you looking to spend?" For example, you may want $375, but they want to spend $400. Let them go first. Then, either agree to their higher price or raise their offer. Get at least what you want or more.

6. The $1,000,000-question to ask is: "Why are you moving?" Investigate their answer.

7. Tell them that you check references, and ask them if their two previous landlords will give them a good recommendation. If they say no, ask WHY? They

Honest Profits

may have a legitimate reason.

8. Now or later, when you are showing the unit, let them know that you do a credit check. Tell them you have a little flexibility, so as not to scare them away, but ask, "What will I find?" This will prove useful later when you do a credit check to see if they are truthful or not. Perform credit checks on all applicants. Check for truthfulness and stability. There are firms that will do this for you, or you can associate with your local credit bureau.

9. Depending on your feeling about them and their interest in the unit, have them drive by and call you back. If they are interested, set up an appointment.

10. If you set up an appointment, do so at your convenience. You run a business, the business doesn't run you. Also, schedule as many appointments at the same time as you can. This saves you time and increases the excitement and interest of prospects if they see that other people want the unit also. Always call an hour or two beforehand to confirm your appointment and remember everyone may not show up.

Being friendly, but firm.

As a landlord, the toughest variable to control is your emotions, unless you follow some pretty hard and fast rules.

Your hardest job if you are renting properties is this: Falling for the hard luck stories of those who miss a rent payment. This is not a time to become lax. It is a time to stick to your guns. If you learn one thing about rental management it's this:

Once tenants get behind they rarely ever catch up!

That's something never to forget.

If tenants get behind on their rent, it is important to tell them immediately:"

The computer shows" [never get personal] that your rental payment is now delinquent. And when that happens we never, and I mean never, ever waver from the rental agreement that you signed.

I'm sorry you're having difficulties meeting the rent. But as the rental agreement says, you must keep up with the rent no matter what. By signing the rental agreement you made that pledge. This is one rule that we must inforce or we'd be out of business."

How to insure your tenants won't be late.

What is greater than love? Stronger than hope?

More powerful than any idea whose time has come?

Well, if it's not a tenant's (and everyone's, for that matter) longing for Recognition and Acknowledgment (R & A), then I don't know what it is.

That's why you should constantly pursue ways to make your tenants (and prospects) feel extra special.

You should try to project that perception and leave the impression that it's not necessarily because they're tenants, but because they are human beings in whom you have a deep and abiding interest. If you're sincere and persistent in your efforts, you'll have an effective advantage over others in real estate that you just might find hard to believe. In fact, your basic employee and tenant policies must foster living and breathing Tender Loving Care ("TLC") techniques. TLC can do wonders to persuade an irrespon-sible tenant to your side and help insure that your tenants pay their rent on time (as well as take good care of your property).

Providing TLC is not just a one-shot, one-tenant event. It's a process that has to be sustained day in and day out. To make it work means you have to be fanatical about every daily transaction, every single hour of every day. It means responding to a tenant's complaint in a timely manner. It means treating every tenant with courtesy. It means not feeling that you're above eating lunch with a low-cost-housing tenant. It means treating everyone you're involved with fairly (yet firmly).

How to give a personality to and humanize an otherwise single dimension business.

You want to tell your responsible tenants that they are valued and that you are sympathetic to their needs—that you'll "be there" when they need you, and that your commitment is ongoing. As I said previously, one marvelous result of this type of action is that many of your responsible tenants will bring even more responsible referrals. I don't have to tell you that once tenants find you to be a pushover on delinquent rent, it doesn't take too long for the word to get around. And what that attracts are irresponsible tenants—which can crowd out the responsible people in no time flat.

Being a good landlord means providing rewards that residents appreciate, such as fresh paint, borders to rooms, ceiling fans, and brass plates (interestingly enough, most tenants are willing to pay for new wallpaper and curtains to match).

If you're having trouble with this philosophy, remember this:

Honest Profits

> ## Robert's Rule:
>
> **It can cost you five times more to get a new tenant than to keep the one you already have.**

That's a documented fact. When a responsible tenant moves, you could spend hundreds of dollars trying to find a responsible replacement. So if someone stays with you for years, you're thousands of dollars ahead. So why not spend a portion of that money on nice gifts such as ceiling fans, mini-blinds, paint, carpeting, etc. Besides, the gifts you give stay with the property and add real value. (Make certain your tenants understand that the gift is for their living enjoyment as long as they stay with you; if they leave, the gift stays with the property.) If tenants stay a year and have been good, reward them with a gift—a ceiling fan or carpet cleaning. It will also enhance the value of your property.

A good financial exercise is to figure the profit over the tenants' lifetime and you'll get an idea of what you can afford to spend to keep them with you. Don't forget, though, all tenants are concerned with is how you can better serve them and meet their exact needs. In other words, how to make their lives better and more fulfilled. That's why my motto is always to give responsible tenants more than they expect.

You are not in the business of renting property. No.

You're in the business of solving problems for people!

Sometimes, a simple, sincere gesture in the form of a thank-you note is sufficient to warm the cockles of even the most irresponsible tenant. More impor-tantly, you don't need to spend a lot of money. The "insider secret" to "getting personal" is to send out notes of congratulations on tenants' birthdays, anniversaries, key holidays, whatever. What this entails is to get this information from your tenants and keep a revolving file that automatically triggers a specific letter. Sure, this takes time. But remember, tenants are your bread and butter—or did you forget who makes it possible for you to eat well on a regular basis?

And, if what I suggest will keep your tenants happy and responsible, they in turn will treat your property like it's their very own—instead of trashing it. Believe me, that's better than good.

On a personal level, one of the best times to start telling people that you appreciate them is during a holiday season. My first choice of when to carry out this effort is at Thanksgiving, since everyone and their mother has something or other circulating in the mails at Christmas. Besides, a "Thank you" at Thanksgiving is quite appropriate. And you don't have to be a brilliant poet to recognize and acknowledge your responsible tenants. A simple, sincere gesture in black and white is generally sufficient.

Here's an example:

Dear _____,

My wife, _____, our daughter _____ (see enclosed photos) and I were out shopping the other evening right after I got home from work, and we decided to look for an appropriate Seasons-Greetings card for you. However, as we got to talking it over, my wife suggested that since this is such a personal time of the year, I should take a few moments out of my hectic twelve-hour day to sit down and write you a personal note. Of course, I realized she was absolutely right.

So, instead of sending you a customary Christmas card, I thought it would be more meaningful if I expressed in my own words how I feel about having you as a tenant.

First of all, I want you to know that I have a high regard for you as a special human being. I feel very fortunate to have you as a tenant. To have the opportunity to know and care for you is a trust I take very seriously. I hope you know that, in the event of any emergency, you can count on me to be there for you at an instant's notice.

You know, it seems that life's richest prizes (and I'm not talking about money) go to the man or woman who values good relationships. I think we all strive to nurture relationships that we can count on to be there when we are in need. As surely as a magnetized piece of steel draws to itself every bit of iron within reach, so does this same force in people draw them closer together when one needs support in emergency situations.

I want to thank you for being a truly responsible tenant, and express my sincere thanks for allowing me to be part of your extended family.

As my holiday gift to you, I've enclosed a gift certificate to _____.

Have a blessed holiday season and a healthy and good new year.

Happy Holidays,

Robert Shemin

P. S. Because I feel very fortunate to have you as a tenant, my mission is to provide you with the best service possible. I can guarantee you this: All of my staff's heart and experience will go into that mission. That's the only way we know.

If you need anything, please ask.

Observe how intimate this letter is. Would the tenant know that I would be there in the event of an emergency situation (not just a minor problem) ? Would it prevent the reader from ever thinking of damaging his or her unit? Wouldn't it prevent the responsible tenant from dropping me as a landlord (what other landlord in the world sends a letter out like this) ?

In today's tumultuous, highly competitive business environment, you have to be different and innovative in order to succeed. You have to develop yourself into a TLC personality so that people can identify with you. Often, that requires a top-to-bottom attitude adjustment from the landlord down to the garbage hauler.

You must think of each and every tenant as a long-term investment.

It's the profit to you over the tenant's lifetime that's important.

You see, a regular Recognition and Acknowledgment (R&A) program can mean that a tenant will stay with you for a long, long time.

For those of you whose greed glands don't buy this "pamp-ering-the-tenant-within-reason" concept—I ask you again to think in terms of the hard dollars you'll lose in rent if you treat your tenants shabbily. Moreover, it's a fact of life that if you don't treat your tenants well, you'll get exactly what you deserve—irresponsible tenants (and their irresponsible friends, significant others, et al) , who could damage your property. Follow the R & A Program. It's good business, and, more importantly, it's the right thing to do.

If you do what's right for your tenants (again, within reason) , you'll begin to receive letters (some will make great testimonials) that you can use when you're interviewing prospective tenants, or when you're applying for a loan, or when you approach a nonprofit group with a joint venture proposal. Those testimonials can go a long way to keep your units occupied, so you'll have more demand for your property than you can ever hope to handle. And that translates into a perpetual source of revenue.

My point: The only way to keep on top of your business and keep the profits you're entitled to is to focus on where your vested interests really lie. And to do that, you have to be painfully honest and timely in how you handle crisis situations.

Robert Shemin's Policies and Procedures.

1. Duties and responsibilities will include:
   - All rent collecting.

- Late notices by the 10th of each month.
- Depositing all rental income
- Rent rolls
- Calling tenants on the 10th to remind them about the rent.

All rent is due on the 1st of every month, and is delinquent (with fees due) on the 5th. More fees accrue on the 10th of the month, and eviction proceedings begin on the 16th. Be very businesslike and polite to all tenants who are late on their rent. Listen to the excuses, but do not acknowledge them. Tell them that your collection processes are business policy, set forth by the owner of the property, and that there are no exceptions. Explain to the late tenants that if they do not bring the rent into your office in a timely fashion, their credit will be marked, and they will be turned over to a collection attorney—always use the name of the eviction attorney.

2. Bookkeeping.
   - Reports on all properties by the 15th of the month.
   - Payroll.
   - All mortgages, bills, etc., to be paid in a timely fashion.
3. Filing and general office management.
4. Telephone renting of units.
   - All rental calls will be answered promptly (same day) and followed up on to make sure tenant is satisfied.
   - Rental calls will be treated as sales calls.
   - A list of potential tenants will be kept at all times.
5. Renting a unit: Sell it. Tell the potential renter that it is a nice unit. Ask callers why they are moving, when they want to move, where they are living now. Ask how the caller heard of the unit.

Never discuss the race of the neighborhoods. If someone asks, say, "I don't know, I am color-blind." If a potential tenant asks about the crime rate in the neighborhood, respond by saying, "We have never had any problems. Any questions concerning that should be directed to the local police department."

6. To show an apartment: Ask the prospective tenants to drive by the property to see if they are interested. Tell the people to call you back if they are interested even if they don't like that particular unit. You may have something else opening soon. Set a time to meet the prospective tenant at the property. Always schedule at least two to three people to meet you at the same time. Mention that you will wait only about five minutes for the person to get there (and never wait more than 15). Be prepared. People often do not show up; but if you have their name and telephone number, call them and ask why they didn't come out. Be sure to make all showings convenient for yourself. That way if someone doesn't show up, you didn't give up anything.

Honest Profits

7. Coordination of Section 8 inspections, leases, etc.
   - Initial inspections.
   - Annual reinspections.
   - Tenant complaints.
   - New leases.
   - Lease renewals.
   - Rent change.
   - Tenant termination.

CHAPTER 6

Right and Wrong Ways to Deal with Contractors

You can come to expect that which you inspect regularly.
Heisenberg's Principle

As I said previously, the successful business is founded on an alliance of self-empowering tenants, suppliers, lenders, and the community at large with a shared interest in the enterprise. The result: long-term loyalty and a staff that will see opportunities for capitalizing on special situations in the marketplace.

I believe in cross-pollination marketing. I'm talking about a winning alliance that uses mutual endorsement as the guiding principle in the relationship. Cross-pollination strategies allow you to tap into a noncompeting firm's identifiable customer base so you have free access to their particular customers. For example, if you know of contractors (as well as bankers, attorneys, accountants, etc.) who have first-hand knowledge of identifiable sources of distressed properties you can have incredible access to finding the best real estate deals. Contractors are often the first to hear about distressed properties. Thus my contractors, bankers, and attorneys bring me deals, and I try to bring them more clients and business.

First and foremost, you have to find a responsible contractor who will charge you a fair price and who will do a first-rate job. No simple task. Your first goal in finding a good contractor is to get the precise information you need to establish the actual value to fix up the home so you can buy it for at least 40% off retail and sell it profitably in today's market. That's why my advice is this:

You must bid every job as if it were your very first and only job!

When dealing with contractors, handymen, and the like, remember this: There are an awful lot of bad apples in the container. So if you're not involved and watching closely you're going to be sorry. Get everything in writing; that way, there is no confusion.

Make sure your contractors are licensed, bonded and insured. Workman's compensation is the national and state system that provides for these people. If workmen get hurt they will be provided for through workmen's compensation

Honest Profits

insurance. If a contractor is not insured, it could cost you a ton of your hard-earned money. That's why it's a sound idea to consult your insurance agent and attorney concerning liability when you're dealing with contractors. Just imagine what will happen to your assets if one of your uninsured workers falls off a roof.

Make it a point to get proof of insurance!

If a contractor does not have it, I deduct the premiums from the money I'm going to pay for the project and buy the workmen's compensation insurance for him.

Quite honestly, I've used people who were not licensed and bonded, and gotten far better prices. There is a lot of risk involved, nevertheless. I recommend that if they are not insured, you send them to your insurance agent. Take out some of their pay and buy the insurance for them. Explain the benefits of this to them.

Mistakes I've made early on in dealing with contractors.

The bottom line is this: You can make or lose a lot of money rehabbing a piece of real estate if you have the wrong contractor doing the work. Many unscrupulous contractors will make the work sound so simple. And their price will sound fair. But, sure enough, they'll end up drinking on the job. Killing time. Overcharging. Failing to show up. Doing shoddy work. Another job takes precedent (they suddenly received cash up front from some unwary client) and they are absent. And you're the stuckee. YOU NEED TO STAY ON TOP OF THEM!

Warning:

Never pay a contractor by the hour. **Never.** That's about as direct to the point as I can get. I've found that if you pay by the hour, all of a sudden a 15-hour paint job takes 50 hours. That's the mindset you could be working with. Therefore, I do the following (see the end of this Section for my Policy and Procedure manual) :
- Only pay by the job.
- Get three competitive written bids.
- Stay continuously on top of them (Heisenberg's Principle).
- Never become dependent on one contractor (let them all know that!)
- Provide very low draws (just enough to cover cost of materials).
- Check that they do good work.
- Don't pay until the work is 100% complete (or it never will get finished). 100% is 100%.
- If work is incomplete beyond a set date, charge a penalty. Time is money. If your property is not ready, then it costs you. Charge the contractor.

I charge a late penalty because I want my contractors to understand that cost

Right and Wrong Ways to Deal with Contractors

savings and quality work permeate every nook and cranny of my company. And they are to provide no exception. I let them know in advance that every day they are not done on time costs me money, either in lost rent or depressed profits. And I don't intend to suffer their irresponsibility alone. In these competitive times, few companies can afford to take even a single contractor for granted and assume they will meet their obligations. Once again, you must stay on top of these people.

Some of you may be wondering where to find contractors. I like to search for people who moonlight, such as roofers who work on weekends to make ends meet. Some real estate people I know drive around and see people working on a roof. They approach the workman and ask, "Are you interested in working on one of my properties on your time off or on weekends?" Sometimes that's all it takes. I've discovered workmen from newspapers, and gotten referrals from property managers, realtors, and friends who've had work done by front-line workmen to an exceptional degree—people with service values who do it right the first time.

Actually, I prefer to work with the same responsible people, for instance: the same heat and air-conditioning person, the same appliance man, the same painter, and so on. I build relationships that work that way. That way you get good dependability and prices (although I do shop them from time to time in order to keep them honest).

So, in the beginning (until you find several that are truly fair and responsible), I suggest you have at least three contractors walk through the details of a house with you. This way you'll learn rather quickly the cost to repair common items of concern such as the central air and heat system, the cost to paint, the cost to carpet, and so on. Try to partner with the contractors.

Here is a list of dos and don'ts for dealing with contractors:

1. Have two to three bids submitted on all work.

2. Hire part-time workers as independent subcontractors responsible for their own insurance and tax requirements.

3. Put clause in contract that independent workers shall not hold you or your company liable for any claims arising from any cause on any job. The liability for each job is the sole responsibility of the bidder alone.

4. Issue check ONLY on completion of job. Regarding draws: Allow a maximum of 1/3 (one-third) of total bid to cover

materials (must provide receipt). Always hold back a substantial portion of payment until after you inspect the job. Mail all checks to recipient.

Make sure you inspect and make sure the following are cleared by the appropriate utility!

a. Electrical after final inspector check.

Honest Profits

    b. Roof after a significant rainfall.
    c. HVAC after five days of continuous operation.
    d. Plumbing after inspecting supply and drainpipes and fixtures.
    e. Trash/hauling after dump receipts and invoices are provided.
    5. Bids.
    a. All bids, without exception, must include the following:
    Start date.

Estimate of time to complete and finish job. Job must be completed on time and in a quality manner. Substandard materials will not be permitted. Disputes over substandard work will be arbitrated by a codes inspector.

- Drugs or alcohol of any kind on job is cause for instant termination.
- Smoking on the job is not permitted. Smoking must take place outside the job area.
- If damage occurs during performance of a job, repairs will be deducted from the bid price.
- Each worker is to submit the following information prior to acceptance of a bid: (a) name (b) driver's license number (c) date of birth (d) Social Security number (e) make, model, and car or truck license number (f) work and home phone number (g) present address (h) three references less than a year old, and (i) proof of workmen's compensation insurance.
- Penalization for nonperformance at $50 per day (including weekends) will be deducted from the contractor's final draw for each day that the job is not completed.
- Penalization for noncompletion that includes any difference in the bid submitted and the cost to complete the job—plus the $50-per-day penalty until the job is completed.

Important:

On Section 8 housing, I hold back twenty percent (20%) of the job total until the unit passes the Section 8 inspection. I also pay a $25 bonus for units that pass the Section 8 inspection the first time.

- Work must be guaranteed for six (6) months.
- Retain first right of refusal, e. g., a bidder who agrees to perform work will not be permitted to subcontract to another party without written permission.
- Bidder must be on job site either by working the project or overseeing his employees.
- Bidder is an independent agent and alone has the responsibility and liability

Right and Wrong Ways to Deal with Contractors

for his workers.
6. Never write or mail a check without a proper invoice.

CHAPTER 7

How to Really Sell a Property

*It's a funny thing about life,
if you refuse to accept anything but the best,
you very often get it.*
W. Somerset Maugham

The Inside Story of How to Really Sell a Property.

You're persistent and you're now at a point where you've fixed up a piece of property, either through your own sweat equity or through hiring contractors. This means you have to make some serious choices depending upon your personal financial goals. You may want to wholesale the property to other investors—which is really a type of equity flipping—or you may want to fix it up and sell it retail to a prospective home buyer (called an end-user). Or you may want to sell it to anyone who'll pay you enough money to make it worth your while. Or, like me, you may want to be a landlord and become independent for the rest of your life on your rental cash flow (while you're building a ton of capital appreciation in the process).

Although hindsight is 20/20, the questions you should have asked yourself before you bought the property are, "What kind of person is going to be interested in living here?" "How will I go about finding prospects?" "Do I currently know anyone who would be interested in owning this real estate?" "Maybe I had better talk to some candidates first to try and determine their level of interest." In my quest for real estate success, these questions save me some hefty dollars in the future.

Straight facts on how to go about finding a buyer for your property.

Let's hope that by now you've compiled a network of private investors and/or nonprofits who are interested in purchasing the type of property you're selling. Yours may be just the type of business opportunity some of these people may want to be let in on.

Also, you may not be aware of it, but every major city has nonprofit organizations that provide low-income houses and dwellings for the homeless and group homes.

Honest Profits

Did you know that some of these homes are in average neighborhoods?

Your mission then, should you accept the assignment, is to find out who are the buyers of these properties. Here's how to find the source of this information:

1. Look in your local newspaper.
2. Take out an ad in the newspaper.
3. Check with realtors.
4. Check with organizations who sponsor group homes.
5. Make a mailing to real estate clubs.
6. Check with prospects you've met at auctions.
7. Use signs, fliers—as many marketing queries as possible. Most people only use one. You should make use of them all.

How to prepare a property for sale.

If you have a property to sell, the idea is to prepare it properly so it has a good chance of selling. We're talking about preparing a house that will have some emotional appeal to prospective buyers, one that can bring a price close to actual market value. Here's how I go about this activity. I conduct little focus groups with the people in the neighborhood. I try to find out what they want. What exactly turns them on? What colors are in? You can also talk to designers, agents, your significant other friends. See what they like. Also, neighbors can sell a house for you. They know people and will talk to people who look at your house.

The high-perceived value items I've found that are particularly helpful in selling a home are the following:

1. Ceiling fans.
2. A brass kick plate.
3. A brass address plate.
4. Bushes.
5. Flowers.
6. Mini-blinds.
7. New toilet seats.
8. Used (they look like new) appliances.
9. Inexpensive alarm systems.
10. Neutral carpeting and colors.

Most people make a decision to buy or rent a home in the time that they enter the front door.

Rest assured that none of the above items are expensive. And the good news is that they'll make your property emotionally more appealing. They enhance your product's desirability and can make your offer more enticing. What's more, it will

How to Really Sell a Property

dramatically show that the property has been properly maintained. Adding these components will also encourage agents to show your property, should you decide to go that route.

WARNING!

Don't over-rehab your property!

That's one of the tricks of the trade I've learned from the most successful pros who've piled up fortunes. It's relevant know-how. The lesson: Don't overspend. That's how many sellers get into deep water.

In an effort to glamorize a property they go overboard and spend far too much because they think it'll increase the value of their property. And they think it will make it easier to sell the property. Too often, rehabbers want the place to look immaculate; everything to be perfect and to their taste.

What they forget is that prospects don't necessarily want to live in the exact house that you live in or the same area you live in. Everyone's looking for different things—although there are some things everyone is looking for.

I work in the low-, moderate-, and middle-income neighbor-hoods. My prospects are looking for nice, clean, fresh places.

And we all know that bathrooms and kitchens sell a property. But that doesn't mean you have to go and spend a fortune on cabinets or vanities. It's far better to maximize your profit by concentrating on basic clean items that work. And again, a little brass, a bit of landscaping, some ceiling fans, and the like can make a big difference in getting a property sold or rented. It all goes back to one critical bottom line element in the success equation:

You make all your money in real estate WHEN YOU BUY IT!

That should be your primary goal. More often than not, that's how people really get rich in real estate. You have to buy it right (at least 40% less than normal market value—and preferably 50% off) in order to sell it to make money.

Buying a property right can overcome almost any marketing obstacle. But a piece of property bought at the wrong price—no matter how you doll it up—can never overcome the handicap of an "off target" purchase price.

SECOND WARNING:

You don't need to overspend to sell a house! That's dumb and costly, and a blunder many people make. Still, all in all, the ability to give your property a higher perceived value than normal market is a vital ingredient in almost any selling effort.

You see, you want to have the amenities fairly nice, neat, and clean so the new

109

occupants can come in and put their finishing (and personal) touch on it. Keeping everything neutral in color is also a key feature.

Ask yourself, "What are the demands in the area?" That's what you really have to learn. And you need first-hand knowledge. For example, here in one of our communities, it seems people like decks attached to their home. So I'll spend an extra $800 and put a deck on a home—and in the process get a lot more money for the property.

Are central air and heat necessary in the community? If so, you can buy a slightly used system. Again, I also use basic and inexpensive carpets for flooring. I've mentioned earlier and I'll mention it again: I'm keen on using inexpensive mini-blinds or window shades in order to make the place look nice. It's a can't-miss way to tempt prospects into making a positive decision. People love them. As a matter of fact, I put in mini-blinds or window shades whenever I buy a property, whether I'm going to sell it or rent it. Another good reason I'm into mini-blinds and window shades is that I want to prevent lookers from peeking in the windows.

Do whatever it will take to sell the property!

But don't go crazy. The point is, you have to determine what it will take to motivate someone to buy your property in today's market—without putting you in a bind. You have to be aware that every dollar you expend can elevate the price of the property, perhaps even above normal market value. The items I've mentioned previously will. A bit of landscaping, some bushes and flowers will surprisingly raise the value of the home, and can bump the amount of your property by at least 5% to 10%.

A lot of people will get a **professional appraisal** before they sell a property, as will people who are seriously considering buying a property. A smart seller wants to set the price below appraisal, while the buyer wants to make sure it's going to appraise higher than the normal market value. More to the point: Put yourself in the buyer's frame of mind when he or she notices that you're asking $5,000 less than the appraised value.

Critical: To attract a prospect's attention I use headlines that promise a benefit—on letters, ads, telemarketing, and any communication I have. Then I measure the results.

The headlines' job: To target the prospect and then get the prospect to read the rest of the copy; and then, finally, to get the prospect to act by sending in a coupon, responding to a phone number, or whatever.

The headline has to hit a prospect like lightning and promise a big believable benefit fast. It must offer an immediate solution so the reader is prompted to act!

A good headline does that. It kind of bends the will of the person who reads or listens to it. That's perfectly natural, because it fills a special human need or want. It may even have an emotional appeal. Somehow a good headline has the right words strung together and hits the reader's hot button (one of his or her needs or desires).

So, what I've constructed for you in the letters and ads I've provided are headlines that literally shout your message out, obscuring other ads on the page.

Remember: The headline that makes it happen is the heart and soul of direct response advertising. By the way, many of my headlines can be used in some adaptive way in your ads. Actually, to attract the greatest number of readers from a Yellow Page ad requires the same prescribed formula and proven techniques as a display ad.

In all of your dealings with prospective buyers, you have to be prepared to offer them a way to save money, save time, and ideally, find the precise benefit they're looking for. Unless you offer an immediate benefit, you will not stir up a prospect's interest and get him or her to act.

Always, always, place yourself in the seat of your potential prospect. Study each individual. Have a dialog, not a monologue. Ask what they're looking for. What turns them on? What turns them off? You can only do this if you get out and look at the neighborhood, schools in the area, playgrounds, crime in the surrounding district, available churches, etc. Look at these things without a fixed point of view to defend. That's tough with some buyers. And it can get even worse if you feel you have to defend your position.

Informal chats with prospects and neighbors can be tough work. But it's the only way I know to help you avoid the real estate pitfalls many professionals still make.

Never assume what the prospect needs or wants until you have asked.

Do your homework.

Never, never show a house until it's absolutely ready to go, and it's ready to be occupied!

And don't worry about being nervous in showing one of your properties. When you show the property, chances are you'll do a better job than a real estate agent. Tell me: Who's in a better position to know it more thoroughly than you? Who's more interested in selling it? Who's researched the area better? Be friendly. Be excited about the property you're offering for sale. Be polite. Be professional. Let the house sell itself.

My strategy is to always have candy, soft drinks, or muffins on hand.

It's also a good idea to have an open house so that all prospects arrive at the same time. Just make it known that you'll be on-site Saturday from 10 a. m. to 2 p. m. or Sunday from 3 p. m. to 5 p. m. It's a way to save yourself five to ten trips back and forth to the property. I found out the hard way that this is an effective way to not only save yourself time showing the property, but hundreds of gallons of gasoline as well.

Your game plan will show lookers that others are interested, which will often prompt a prospect to make an immediate decision. My experience has shown that it's also a good idea to let people know that "This property is going to go quickly."

A simple postcard mailing can bring in more investors than you can hope to handle.

Here's a neat little trick. It will point out just how valuable your prospect list is. What you need to get started is:

1. Your up-to-date mailing list that has the names and addresses of all of the potential buyers you've collected.

2. A supply of inexpensive postcards.

3. An answering machine that will let you record a message at least two minutes in length.

Stick one of your postcards into a typewriter and type a message that reads something like this:

Dear Friend,

Would you like to learn about a house that I have for sale, at below market value, that's truly an exceptional bargain? Fact is, it seems incredible that I can offer this house for this price.

If you would like to learn more, all you have to do is call 000-0000 to hear a FREE recorded message. It will reveal probably the best piece of real estate to be offered in a long time.

Sincerely,

Robert Shemin, Esq.

Next, have all your postcards printed up with the same message (I like to send out pink postcards. It gets the recipients' attention fast). Now address them to everybody on your list.

Then you've got to write out a little telephone script. It might read like this:

"Thank you for calling. My name is Robert Shemin. I've been involved in the community here for ten years and I'm proud to say I know many of my neighbors personally. As a result, from time to time I find a wonderful piece of property with great potential, spend the necessary money to get it in really good condition, and then sell it for a modest profit. If you are interested, I'm sure we can work out the terms that fit your budget best. That's my job. I look forward to meeting you soon and talking to you about financing, points, and closing. Please call me at 000-0000 and tell me when you're available and we'll get together so you can see what a wonderful bargain I have in store for you. Of course, there is no obligation whatsoever."

How to Really Sell a Property

Practice reading the script a few times and then record it on your answering machine. Then all you have to do is mail your postcards and sit back and wait for the phone to ring off the hook. I'll tell you why this works so well:

1. It presents a bargain and perhaps financial security.
2. It's totally nonthreatening to a prospect.
3. It offers an easy way to get free information.
4. The caller listens to a voice that sounds sincere, trustworthy, and caring.
5. They know they can't get ripped off.
6. And finally, you offer a no-risk, no-obligation-whatsoever proposition.

Marketers know that people often have a stronger desire to avert loss than to gain a potential advantage. What people typically try to avoid is being ripped off (financial loss), emotional pain, wasting time and worry. The reason this marketing concept works is that you're dealing with basic human appeals. The trick is to experiment and discover what appeal is best for your particular business.

The above technique can work no matter what kind of offer you want to make.

For example, let's say you're looking for real estate to purchase. All you have to do is change the wording around a bit and, lo and behold, you can adapt it to almost any situation, to: For Sale By Owner, real estate purchase for cash regardless of condition, and so forth.

You may also want to try running a small "postcard ad" in your local paper. All it requires is a small change in the "look" of the copy. Here's an example:

Want to buy a house at below market value, that's truly an exceptional bargain?

It seems incredible that I can offer this house for this price. Call (000) -0000 for an amazing FREE recorded message. Call anytime, 24 hours a day.

Pretty simple formula. Why not use it? One of the secrets to my success is this:

I avoid ever having a prospect perceive that there is risk in doing business with me.

I talk benefits to the prospect. I educate. I offer multiple options. I offer to do all the document work. I offer something free. I romance people by stressing my personal service. I create the impression that I'm the one at risk.

If you really want to get attention, here are a few more suggested ads that are sure to bring out highly motivated buyers in droves. Fact is, these ads will pull better than your competitors'— even the biggest ones in town.

Local Property Expert Discovers New Way to Sell Your Distressed Property at Top Dollar. Call (000) -0000 for an amazing FREE recorded message. Call anytime, 24 hours a day.

Honest Profits

> Divorce Forces Local Owner to Practically Give Away This House. Call 000-0000 for an appointment anytime, 24 hours a day.

Note: You could substitute for divorce such words as Banker or Money Problems.

> Local Real Estate Owner Swears Under Oath He Did Not Steal House He's Selling So Cheaply. Call (000) -0000 for an appointment. Call anytime, 24 hours a day.

> Marketing Genius Looking for Distressed Properties to Market. Call 000-0000 for an appointment. Call 24 hours a day.

> Would You Like to Trade the Equity in Your House for Another House? Call 000-0000 for an appointment. Call 24 hours a day.

> Would You Like a Low-Risk Investment That Can Bring You a 20% Annualized Return? Call 000-0000 for an appointment. Call 24 hours a day.

> THIS HOUSE IS A REAL STEAL. GOING THROUGH BANKRUPTCY. Call 000-0000 for an appointment. Call 24 hours a day.

> FORECLOSURE FOR SALE. Comparable houses on block going for $15,000 more. This property going for 25% less per square foot than others. Call

How to Really Sell a Property

Here are are the steps you must take in order to sell a piece of property that can generate the kind of profits you're looking for:

1. To Sell Retail or Wholesale to Investors:

   a. Have you done proper "due diligence" and determined in advance if the property is, indeed, marketable?

   b. Have you determined in advance who you are going to sell the property to? How you are going to advertise it? How it will be financed? The closing costs and interest rate?

   c. Is the property located in a neighborhood where houses sell easily? Is the price of the real estate higher or lower than surrounding properties? Is it in "marketable shape"?

   d. Would you buy it? If not, are the terms really a "good deal" from a buyer's perception?

   e. Is there a low-enough cash requirement to make this property attractive?

   f. Have you added specific high-perceived value enhancements such as ceiling fans, carpet, paint, etc. ?

   g. Have you considered the long-term value of quickly turning the property over for even a small profit?

   h. Have you considered all creative alternatives to make the sale viable, such as offering:

- To pay all closing costs.
- A lease to own option.
- A purchase to cover the down payment.
- A barter or exchange for other real estate.
- A special rebate
- To split down payment

   i. Have you taken into consideration these 10 powerful and profitable owner-financing selling strategies (and caveats) ?

- Don't transfer title until your due diligence is complete.
- Get the deed in escrow if at all possible.
- Use a wrap-around mortgage strategy.
- Sell all or a portion of the mortgage for cash.
- Offer relatively low monthly payments with a short-term balloon (one to five years).
- Offer an easy monthly payment plan with lump-sum interval payments.
- Barter for real estate.

Honest Profits

- Sell all or part of the mortgage for immediate cash.

j. Have you included these essential clauses in the contract?

- Personal guarantee of parties involved.
- Late fee.
- Balloon.
- Collection
- Rent assignment.
- Clause covering who pays attorney fees.

k. Have you prepared an attractive "fact sheet"? (See Appendix.)

2. Here's how to find motivated investors:

a. Advertise to real estate clubs.

b. Advertise in the newspaper (three excellent headlines are "Going Through Bankruptcy—A Real Steal!" and "Foreclosure for Sale!")

The ideal ad should contain the following information:

- Owner financing, payment, down payment, special terms, who pays closing costs.
- Location.
- Number of bedrooms, bathrooms special amenities.
- Square feet of property.

c. Talk to realtors, friends, attorneys, accountants.

d. Use direct-response marketing.

- Acquire (and begin to compile) mailing lists of owner/ prospects, churches, auction attendees, and real estate club members.
- Send letter to all of the above announcing your offer. (See below.)

3. How to handle prospects who respond to your ads and direct mail:

a. When possible (unless your ad specifies otherwise) handle all calls personally.

b. Capture every prospect name, address, phone number, and job status for your mailing list.

c. Determine quickly what the caller is seeking.

d. Be educational and avoid forceful sales techniques.

e. Make every effort to qualify the prospect in advance.

f. If you are satisfied you have qualified the prospect, provide him or her with the property address.

g. Alert a neighbor that the prospect is arriving at a specific timeagreed upon in advance (often the prospect is late), and ask if you may leave the key.

h. Call the prospect within the next 24 hours to determine interest.

4. How to deal with realtors:

a. Ask for a reduced rate if you are required to pay for the advertising. Get the ad schedule in writing.

b. Sign a 90-day agreement.

Get a buyout agreement.

c. Use an exclusive agency.

A final word of W A R N I N G:

Would you loan someone, anyone, even a friend, $50,000 without first running a credit check?

Of course you wouldn't. You must run a credit check on anyone seriously interested in buying your property. Yet that's just what a number of sellers don't do. Think of it as an evaluation of your buyer. If you don't, the contents of that report could come back to haunt you. Check with a property manager in your area to find a reliable firm.

Use one that does credit checks. Over 50% of all real estate contracts fail because the buyer cannot get a loan.

Make sure that your buyer is prequalified by a bank or a mortgage company before you spend or waste time showing a house or negotiating a contract. It's also good for the buyer if he/she is prequalified. It will save him or her a lot of frustration, and it's good for your network. Develop a good relationship with a mortgage company or bank who will prequalify your prospects; and perhaps these contacts can help you by sending you deals, buyers, and/or loaning you money. **An Effective Letter to Locate Investors**

This is a sample of a letter you can send to real estate club members. It can work far better if you yourself are a member of the club and can say so in the letter.

Dear Investor (Personalized),

Because I am a member of the Nashville Real Estate Club, I believe that you and I can structure a project that will net you, at the very least, $10,000, but more likely $25,000 or more in bottom line profits.

Actually I'm willing to take all of the risk on this project.

I'll call you in the next few days and spend 10 minutes reviewing the details of the offer.

Assuming you have an interest, I will work out all of the details with you to move ahead on this exciting project.

I do look forward to working with you, and I trust we can set up an appointment at your earliest convenience.

I hope, for both our sakes, that you're available for this project.

Sincerely,

Your Name

P. S. Either this project will make dollars and sense to you or it won't. I think it will. The reason: Most of the missing pieces are now in place to make it happen. This truly is an extraordinary situation. But, then, you can be the judge.

LETTER TO POTENTIAL INVESTOR TO SELL A PROPERTY

You can try a number of versions of this offer geared to any number of different types of investors, e. g., real estate club members, nonprofits, etc.

Dear _____,

I'm writing to urge you to take immediate action on a wonderful opportunity that just became available.

Here's what it's all about:

I have a piece of property that I've purchased recently, that almost any astute, no-nonsense investor would find an exceptional value. I have completely rehabilitated the house and would welcome your inspection of any structural portion or mechanical system of the property. There are no serious defects and the asking price is well below normal market value.

It is my opinion that, over any number of years of ownership, this property is going to give someone the peace of mind of having made a very sound financial investment.

I will give you a call in the next few days to see if you have an interest. If you want even more prompt action, my telephone number is 000-0000. Or, if you

How to Really Sell a Property

would prefer, I have prepared a fact sheet on this property and will send it to you upon request.

If I can be of help to you in answering any questions you might have regarding this property, please call me. I will also include a bit of information about the work that we do in the _____ area, the people we help, and the solutions we provide for individuals and nonprofit organizations.

By the way, I realize that you may not know me, but I am familiar with your community. And as a member of the community, I should tell you that the kind of relationship I am seeking, regardless of whether you have an interest in this property or not, is a long and enduring one. I really only want to sell you something that meets your precise needs.

Fact is, from time to time I'd be happy just to show you some of the unique properties I uncover in the marketplace that go unrecognized. And, of course, I won't be offended if you buy from someone else. Actually, I may advise you against certain properties even though it might be in my interest to do otherwise.

It is the long-term relationship that meets the test of time that I'm interested in maintaining.

I can also assure you that I will make available my best deals even if we never make contact again. And I will make sure that the only situations I show you are those that are in your best interest. I don't want you ever to make any errors, and, frankly, I don't want to make any myself.

Sincerely,

Your Name

Here's a suggested telescript to follow up with:
"Mr. Jones, this is Sally Robbins.
I am calling you to see if you received the letter I sent regarding a piece of property that is now available, and whether you had any questions about it. I am on a tight schedule, but I would be delighted to take the time to answer any questions you might have regarding the property. "

Honest Profits

LETTER TO INVESTORS TO FLIP A PIECE OF PROPERTY

This is a letter to investors on your list that you believe will have an interest in rehabilitating a piece of property that you've picked up for a literal "song." And since you're in need of cash, you've decided to quickly turn the property. A "penny" letter is ideal for this situation. The following opening is from *The Robert Collier Letter Book*, by Robert Collier (Prentice-Hall, Inc.). Please check your local library for a copy. It is, in my opinion, the best book on copyrighting that I've ever read.

You'll notice that this letter also takes the reader into your confidence and tells him or her why you are putting the property up for sale. That's a critical component of a good direct mail piece.

(ATTACH PENNY HERE WITH CLEAR TAPE.)

Dear Friend,

It's a wonderful thing—the power of money to make money. Just this little, insignificant penny invested at the birth of Christ, at an interest rate of only 4% compounded semi-annually, would today amount to more than $200,000,000,000,000,000,000—many times the wealth of the world!

It's too late now to backdate your investments to then, but you can do the next best thing. You can take a hard look at a house that I've just purchased. You could rehab it, and I believe you would achieve a $10,000 or even a $15,000 personal payoff for the effort.

In my view there are few potential problems and no serious defects in this property. It is structurally and mechanically sound. But you and your appraisers can be the judge.

My ulterior motive in wanting to turn this property is simply that at this moment in time my plate is full and my contractors are up to their elbows in work. I am also not in a cash flow position to take on even one more exceptional opportunity. As a result, my options are either to shelve it for a few months or quickly turn it. I've decided to do the latter.

I can assure you that with the proper rehabbing this property could bring an excellent asking price. Again, you be the judge.

If you have an interest, please call my office at 000-0000. It's first come first served on this exceptional offering. This really is a "sleep well at night" investment that comes along once in a blue moon.

Sincerely,

Your Name

"To-Do" List When Preparing to Sell a Property

EXTERIOR: Landscaping should look presentable. Trim all trees and shrubs. Clean up lawn (i. e. , rake leaves, mow, etc.). Edge driveway. Install shutters. Install large house numbers on front of home. Decorative front door (or repaint). Paint using semi-gloss (paint front first). Install new windows if needed (in front first).

KITCHEN: Be certain sink is clean and looks present-able. Install cabinet fronts with new knobs. Install wallpaper with adequate borders. Hang or place a deodorizer. Install bright new linoleum on floor. Install decorative wall plugs. Appliances are not mandatory but add value. Install ceiling fans and mini-blinds. Install a working smoke/fire alarm.

BEDROOMS & BATHROOMS. Paint trim in semi-gloss with different colors. If necessary, refinish tub/shower and sink. Consider cedar in all closets. Install neutral wallpaper with borders or paint. Install a ceiling fan (use light fixture if applicable). If necessary, marolite over damaged walls. Don't strip wood or restain. Replace outdated faucets. Install mini-blinds. Install new shower curtain. If needed, install carpet and pad. Use denture tablets or similar item to clean toilets.

LIVING ROOM: Install molding at ceiling. If appropriate, use some decorative paneling. Professionally install carpet and padding. Install inexpensive curtains or mini-blinds. Install ceiling fans (use light fixture if applicable).

CHAPTER 8

Success

Bigness comes from doing many small things well.
R. H. Macy

*Luck is
where preparation meets opportunity.*
Anonymous

Quick Points on Being Successful.

Get a separate phone line, answering machine, or service. Return all phone calls within four hours and always respond to all calls the same day you receive them. Even if you cannot talk, acknowledge the call. This will put you ahead of 95% of your competition. I find good deals because I am usually the first to call.

My places stay rented because I or my assistant return calls. Many tenants tell me that they called dozens of places, but I was the first and only one to call back.

Be persistent. If I need to talk to prospects I will call them every day, sometimes twice a day, until we talk.

Be organized. Get a daily calendar. Write things down. Keep good notes. Be able to go back and look things up in your files. My files consist of:
- Investment possibilities.
- A file for each property with all documents and notes about it.
- A hot sheet list of potential investment (wholesale) buyers and retail buyers with their names, addresses, preferences, phone and fax numbers. I constantly update and add to this list.
- A "To Do Today" file.
- Tenant files which are constantly updated. If you have a computer, use it. Develop marketing lists. Stay in contact.

Get a separate banking account to keep track of your real estate investing. This will help you prepare for tax season. Keep all checks and receipts. Be able to account for everything.

Remember—you will have your own business. You can write off a lot of expenses, business travel and meals, office supplies, a possible home office, a car driven for

Honest Profits

business purposes (keep a log of miles).

Always carry a file with contracts and leases ready to be signed.

More on Success.

Some deals may take months, or even years. People who do not sell or buy may do so later. Keep track of everyone and everything for at least four years. Review old files and possible investments every few months. Make those phone calls and visits again. I have bought houses that I first looked at three years ago. It took that long for the sellers to come around, or perhaps conditions changed.

Be nice to everyone, regardless of position. Two of my best deals came from a drug-addict janitor. I saw him cleaning up at the convention center here. Because I was friendly toward him, I was able to buy two houses from him. I helped save him thousands of dollars he would have lost from a foreclosure, and kept him from becoming homeless. And he helped me make thousands of dollars on the good deals.

Be patient. Wait for the really good deals. If one slips by or you lose a few, don't worry. Another, better deal will come along.

If you don't lose on a deal every now and then, you are probably not doing enough deals. I have lost some money before, but I learned great lessons.

Be sure to take a break every now and then. Just like any other business, especially if it is your own, it can get very busy. It is fun and exciting. I work a lot of evenings and weekends, but everyone must take a break.

Know your priorities. You can create an enormous amount of wealth through real estate, but real wealth lies in your relationships. Relationships with God, yourself, your family, and your friends are your true riches. I have made $5,000 in a few days, but nothing comes close to the joy my wife and child give me daily. One second of seeing my child smile is worth more than all of my real estate and material wealth. What are your priorities?

Have fun. If it is not enjoyable, do not do it.

Help people first, make money second. If you cannot help people, it probably is not worth doing. I provide quality low-income housing to help people and to make money. Many times I have bought houses that were being foreclosed on. At foreclosure, the owners would get nothing. I often pay them tens of thousands of dollars, helping them find a new home and save their credit. I help them and I make a profit.

You are self-employed. Enjoy it. Dress as you like. Do not worry about impressing people. Oftentimes I go downtown in shorts and a fun T-shirt, driving my plain car. Many of the bankers, lawyers, and professionals look at me like I am some kind of bum. I think it is funny. I do not have to wear a suit and tie to work and take only two weeks of vacation a year, yet I probably make more in three months than they make all year.

Take a long-term approach to your business. Be in it for the long term. And remember your long-term goals. It is possible to get rich quick, but highly unlikely. Though I had many successes in the first six months I got into real estate, it took about two years to really hit my stride.

Here's an enormous selling edge nobody ever told you about that will allow you to strike pay dirt year after year.

A vital key to your success is to begin immediately to compile a prospect list of real estate agents, potential investors, attorneys, accountants, non-profits, lending institutions, etc. , to whom you send regular letters (personalized computer-generated letters will outpull a "Dear Occupant" letter by as much as 400%) .

It's always amazing to me that people in real estate who have acquired this information over the years do not take advantage of it. If you want to win this race called life, you must continually focus your mind on the real task out there, which is to shape up your prospect list. The short- and long-term payoff can be phenomenal.

My advice is quickly to get a vital "on target" OPERATING SYSTEM in place (later, you can hire an outside service) and start every work week making sure that you run two to three ads to locate properties, offer free special reports, send out 100 letters to locate properties, send personalized letters to tenants, send out letters to 100 potential investors, 100 real estate agents, 100 nonprofits, 100 For Sale By Owner properties, 100 contractors, 50 loan officers, and so forth. Follow up each mailing with a telemarketing campaign. (Telemarketing, even at a basic level, works like crazy, and when coupled with direct mail can increase your response up to 400%.) Be systematic and persistent, and do not limit yourself. You can do more.

Also make sure that within each seven-day time period you will approach ten people with offers.

The above OPERATING SYSTEM allows you to have a perpetual stream of prospects contacting you. The point: To have an ongoing efficient system in place that's operating and working for you every single day of the week. Then, once you've determined what works for you in your particular area, you can do more of the same.

If you want to look to the future with confidence and profit accordingly, then my philosophy, *and this is critical,* is this:

TO TAKE THE GUESSWORK OUT OF REAL ESTATE INVESTMENTS:

Never, ever buy a house unless you *know* it is 40% below market value!

Honest Profits

Be forewarned: I heavily emphasized that statement for good reason. You make or lose money in real estate when you BUY.

None of us are geniuses as far as I know. You want an edge. You want to avoid traps. You want a cushion in case your financial analysis of the property is in error.

At this point you may be saying to yourself, "But I didn't have to pay good money to have someone tell me that the way to real estate wealth is to buy properties at 40% below market. Anybody could have told me that!"

The point I'm trying to make is this: While it may be somewhat difficult to find such properties, they do exist. And I'm here to tell you how to find them.

So listen to me again:

The most important decision you will ever make in real estate is the purchase price!

This is the part you have to get right. That's why my 40% to 50% rule is so crucial to your success. It will save you in the event that your estimates are off. That's also why with up-to-date information and analysis you can make a killing. Otherwise, you can lose your shirt.

Critically important:

You have to buy a property right, because the last thing you want is to be constantly weathering cash-flow storms or "hidden" disasters. You want to keep small problems small. What you should be looking for, no matter how long it takes, is to turn someone else's crisis into your opportunity.

Buying properties at least 40% below market value will allow you to execute the kind of future strategies that lead to success and sustain growth—growth you can control and maintain year after year. Then you can be almost guaranteed a predictable stream of earnings. In other words, you want a "can't miss" growth situation.

Unemotional discipline is the name of the game

Sure, you'll be tempted to buy certain properties. Stick with your game plan and remember that a first-rate real estate mind requires a participant/observer outlook: A viewpoint that enables you to view each deal from both a first-person perspective (your day-to-day living) and a third-person perspective.

A 20% to 30% return on investment is not for me!

That may be a good deal for you. It's not for me. I'm ultraconservative by nature. I need a cushion. If I'm going to buy a house, fix it up, and sell it, I need at the very minimum to buy it at 40% below market. Fact is, 50% below is what I'm really looking for. Do you know why? It's because I start out with the basic assumption that there are going to be some hidden costs I've overlooked. That doesn't always happen, of course. But it can. I also begin every deal on the premise that real estate can be a risky business. I don't like risk. I want to avoid risk and any sudden changes in the economy that might otherwise spell financial disaster. I want to grow and enjoy increasing profits. The only way to accomplish my goals is to avoid risk by buying a property at 50% of its retail price, give or take a few points of its value. Only then can I make the kind of money that I'm looking for.

With almost any piece of property, you have to realize that (with very few exceptions), there are going to be numerous minor things that will go wrong. There will be some surprise hidden repair costs you've never anticipated. Also, some rental property is not easy to sell, if and when you want to get out.

If you have a large enough spread, these particular problems will cause you no major concern.

That's why you must make sure you run an accurate cash-flow projection

on every piece of property you intend to buy.

That's critical. You have to know what the property is going to cost you. Talk to contractors and other experts in the field. Project the expenses you're going to have, such as: Appraisal cost. Termite letters. Surveys. Your monthly payments until you sell it. Property taxes. Insurance. Utilities. Closing costs. Commissions. Advertising expense, if you intend to sell the property. Finders' fees. In other words, you need to calculate every penny that's going to come out of your pocket before you do anything with the property.

Important: You have to include all of the above expenses in your cash-flow and profit-and-loss projections if you're going to rent the property; buy it and flip it; or buy it, fix it up, and sell it.

Here are the steps for gaining profits even during periods of heavy competition, or during any critical new industry trends.

a. Draft an action plan in advance that keys in on the personal needs and objectives of the seller. It is critical that you know how the seller will personally win by getting the results that you can deliver.

b. Determine the "red flags" that could kill the deal, and either reduce or eliminate them in advance.

c. Establish an early win/win financial strategy so that the seller can quickly see you as a partner in his or her success rather than as an opponent to be overcome. This is a key element in the sale.

d. Take an efficient and professional approach and try to seek out everyone's actual position in the selling decision.

e. Never be forceful or overbearing. The seller should view your proposal or options as a logical conclusion to be drawn from the data provided. It is your professional approach to working toward *a winning result for all parties* that will set you apart from the competition.

Honest Profits

f. Ask questions that are geared to solving the seller's personal or financial problem. Your goal is to get below the tip of the iceberg to the solution at hand. Play the game of 1000 questions.

g. Determine how receptive the seller is to the "What if I could give you X in cash today? What is your downside limit?" approach. If you stay with statements such as, "The data shows such and such . . . .", or "Our strategic analysis shows the following . . ." then the data becomes the disinterested third party, and personality conflict is eliminated. Thus your current position and the seller's specific objectives can be better accomplished while untenable positions are eliminated.

Set your goals. Plan how to get there, and go for it.

Eat right and exercise. Try not to eat anything artificial. Exercise for 30 minutes to an hour, three or four times a week. It is great for the body and the mind. It is my time, my break.

Always learn. Take classes. Get more degrees. Go to seminars and speeches. I learn new things all of the time. Talk to older people who have done what you are doing. Learn from their successes and mistakes.

Share your experiences with a relative, a loved one, or a friend. It is a lot more fun to ride around and look at properties with someone.

Perform a random act of kindness daily. Be extra polite. Help someone with a package. Make a elderly person smile. Give an unexpected gift.

The rewards are infinite.

CHAPTER 9

Action Plan

Chapter 1 Action List

What do you need to get started?

Find and attend two auctions this month. They are advertised in the real estate section of your paper. Or call local auction companies.

Look in the Sunday paper every Sunday. Circle all For Sale By Owner properties and all investment properties. Call on owners, talk to sellers—look and learn.

WEEK ONE

Call your HUD and VA office, get lists of all properties for sale, if any, and look at four HUD or VA properties over the next four weeks.

Begin to collect and update all of your financial data: savings, income, assets, and expenses. Find your tax returns.

WEEK TWO

Take two hours on Saturday. Find an area of town that is what we call "in transition" (not a great neighborhood, not a horrible neighborhood, but one that is being fixed up) and drive around it. Copy all FSBO signs, take down at least five For Sale by real estate agent signs, and call those people. Look at at least five houses in the neighborhood. Learn your way around. See what the houses look like; estimate their value, and start attempting to determine which ones are undervalued. Repeat this every Saturday for four weeks.

Contact three real estate agents from three large companies. Tell them you are looking for undervalued properties that can either be fixed up and sold or fixed up and rented out. Also ask them for nonqualifying loans on houses. Have them show you at least five properties in the next five weeks.

Call the local tax assessor's office. Find out when the next tax sale will be. Learn all you can about the tax sale and attend one tax sale auction in the next year.

Call an attorney and find out in what publications foreclosures are publicized in your area. Get at least one of these publications. Use this guide and any help you can find to understand and analyze the foreclosure notices.

Call one major bank, one major mortgage company, and one second mortgage company and find the right person—whether it be through the real estate owned (REO) department or special asset department—and find out about any real estate for sale. Contact the appropriate lending institutions in the next three weeks and get their lists of properties.

Call two real estate auction companies and get on their mailing lists.

Start taking classes to become a licensed real estate agent within 30 days.

Join your local real estate investment club.

Go to an auction and meet at least two other real estate investors. Get their phone numbers, fax numbers, and addresses, and make note of the types of properties they buy. Take them out to lunch and ask them about their businesses and whether they'll show you some of their properties. You'll be amazed at what they'll reveal to you.

Find two good and reputable contractors in your local area. Get to know them. Find out about all of their skills. Try to enlist them as bird dogs, offering them rewards when you close on a deal they found.

Enlist at least three bird dogs in the next six weeks.

Fill out the financial statement in the back of this book, or go to your bank and fill out theirs. Get your credit report.

WEEK THREE

Put together a nice-looking financial package for a bank. It should include your financial statement, resume, etc. It will look, feel, and be impressive.

WEEK FOUR

Have a bank review your package. Ask for feedback.

Review and fill out a sample land trust this week.

Review and fill out two sample real estate contracts this week.

Get two copies of real estate contracts from your local Board of Realtors, a real estate agent and/or attorney. Compare them to the contracts in this book.

Get a free initial consultation with your local attorney to discuss how you should title your property. Also find out whether you need a property management company, if you are going to be a landlord.

Meet with your accountant within three weeks to discuss the tax implications of using a land trust, limited partnership, or corporation.

Make five extremely low offers, presented in contract form, with your weasel clause and 90 days to close in the next 10 days. Make sure they are LOW offers; and

Action Plan

if they are accepted, read Chapter Five on Turning Real Estate into Profits.

If you and your advisors determine that you should incorporate or form a partnership, do so within 30 days.

Put your own home in a trust and record it at the courthouse. Advise your insurance company, mortgage company, and tax assessor.

Check with your insurance company to see if you need to change the titling or type of your insurance policy as you begin a successful real estate business.

Keep looking for and finding deals. Flip them, keep them, lease option them, rent them out, reatil sell them. Prosper and have fun. Please let me know your name and address so you can be put on my mailing list.

Free Special Report $19.99 Value.

25 Costliest Mistakes Almost All Investors Make And How To Avoid Them.

Name _____

Address _____

City, State _____

Zip Code _____

Phone: _____

To:
Robert Shemin
P.O. Box 128186
Nashville, TN 37212-8186

131

Appendix

Please feel free to use or copy any of the enclosed letters or forms. Remember to please consult your attorney and/or accountant before relying upon these documents or any of the information contained in these materials. Happy investing. Have fun. Do it with a conscience.

308 NEIL AVENUE TRUST

THIS AGREEMENT AND DECLARATION OF TRUST is made and entered into this _____ day of October, 1993, by and between **Robert D. Shemin**, as Grantors and Beneficiary, (hereinafter referred to as the "Beneficiary" or "Beneficiaries", whether one or more, which designation shall include all successors in interest of any beneficiary) **YOUR NAME AND ADDRESS** (hereinafter referred to as the "Trustee", which designation shall include all successor trustees).

IT IS MUTUALLY AGREED AS FOLLOWS:

1. **Trust Property**. The Beneficiary is about to convey or cause to be conveyed to the Trustee by deed, absolute in form, the property described in the attached **Exhibit "A"**, which said property shall be held by the Trustee, in trust, for the following uses and purposes, under the terms of this Agreement and shall be hereinafter referred to as the "Trust Property".

2. **Consideration**. No consideration has been paid by Trustee for such conveyance. The conveyance will be accepted and will be held by Trustee subject to all existing encumbrances, easements, restrictions or other clouds or claims against the title thereto, whether the same are of record or otherwise. The property will be held on the trusts, terms and conditions and for the purposes hereinafter set forth, until the whole of the trust estate is conveyed, free of this trust, as hereinafter provided.

3. **Beneficiary**. The person(s) named in the attached **Exhibit B"** are the Beneficiary(ies) of this Trust (referred to as "Beneficiary" or "Beneficiaries"), and as such, shall be entitled to all of the earnings, avails and proceeds of the Trust Property according to their interests set opposite their respective names.

4. **Interests**. The interests of the Beneficiary shall consist solely of the following rights respecting the Trust Property:

    a. The right to direct the Trustee to convey or otherwise deal with the title to the Trust Property as hereinafter set out.

    b. The right to manage and control the Trust Property.

    c. The right to receive the proceeds and avails from the rental, sale, mortgage, or other disposition of the Trust Property.

The foregoing rights shall be deemed to be personal property and may be assigned and otherwise transferred as such. No Beneficiary shall have any legal or equitable right, title or interest, as realty, in or to any real estate held in trust under this Agreement, or the right to require partition of that real estate, but shall have only the rights, as personalty, set out above, and the death of a Beneficiary shall not terminate this Trust or in any manner affect the powers of the Trustee.

5. **Power of Trustee**.

   a. With the consent of the Beneficiary, the Trustee shall have authority to issue notes or bonds and to secure the payment of the same by mortgaging the whole or any part of the Trust Property; to borrow money, giving notes therefor signed by him in his capacity as Trustee; to invest such part of the capital and the profits therefrom and the proceeds of the sale of bonds and notes in such real estate, equities in real estate, and mortgages in real estate in the United States of America, as he may deem advisable.

   b. With the consent of the Beneficiary, the Trustee shall have the authority to hold the legal title to all of the Trust Property, and shall have the exclusive management and control of the properly as if he were the absolute owner thereof, and the Trustee is hereby given full power to do all things and perform all acts which in his judgment are necessary and proper for the protection of the Trust Property and for the interest of the Beneficiary in the property of the Trust, subject to the restrictions, terms, and conditions herein set forth.

   c. Without prejudice to the general powers conferred on the Trustee hereunder, it is hereby declared that the Trustee shall have the following powers, with the consent of the Beneficiary:

   (1) To purchase any real property for the Trust at such times and on such terms as may seem advisable; to assume mortgages upon the property.

   (2) To sell at public auction or private sale, to barter, to exchange, or to otherwise dispose of, any part, or the whole of the Trust Property which may from time to time form part of the Trust estate, subject to such restrictions and for such consideration for cash and/or for credit, and generally upon such terms and conditions as may seem judicious, to secure payment upon any loan or

2

loans of the Trust, by mortgage with or without power of sale, and to include such provisions, terms, and conditions as may seem desirable.

(3) To rent or lease the whole or any part of the Trust Property for long or short terms, but not for terms exceeding the term of the Trust then remaining.

(4) To repair, alter, tear down, add to, or erect any building or buildings upon land belonging to the Trust; to fill, grade, drain, improve, and otherwise develop any land belonging to the Trust; to carry on, operate, or manage any building, apartment house, or hotel belonging to the Trust.

(5) To make, execute, acknowledge, and deliver all deeds, releases, mortgages, leases, contracts, agreements, instruments, and other obligations of whatsoever nature relating to the Trust Property, and generally to have full power to do all things and perform all acts necessary to make the instruments proper and legal.

(6) To collect notes, obligations, dividends, and all other payments that may be due and payable to the Trust; to deposit the proceeds thereof, as well as any other monies from whatsoever source they may be derived, in any suitable bank or depository. and to draw the same from time to time for the purposes herein provided.

(7) To pay all lawful taxes and assessments and the necessary expenses of the Trust, to employ such officers, brokers, engineers, architects, carpenters, contractors, agents, counsel, and such other persons as may seem expedient, to designate their duties and fix their compensation; to fix a reasonable compensation for their own services to the Trust, as organizers thereof.

(8) To represent the Trust and the Beneficiary in all suits and legal proceedings relating to the Trust Property in any court of law of equity, or before any other bodies or tribunals; to begin suits and to prosecute them to final judgment or decree; to compromise claims or suits, and to submit the

3

same to arbitration when, in their judgment, such course is necessary or proper.

(9) To arrange and pay for and keep in force in the name and for the benefit of the Trustee, such insurance as the Trustee may deem advisable, in such companies, in such amounts, and against such risks as determined necessary by the Trustee.

6. **Duties of Trustee**. It shall be the duty of the Trustee in addition to the other duties herein imposed upon him:

a. To keep a careful and complete record of all the beneficial interests in the Trust Property with the name and residence of the person or persons owning such beneficial interest, and such other items as they may deem of importance or as may be required by the Beneficiary.

b. To keep careful and accurate books showing the receipts and disbursements of the Trust and also of the Trust Property, and such other items as he may deem of importance or as the Beneficiary hereunder may require.

c. To keep books of the Trust open to the inspection of the Beneficiary at such reasonable times at the main office of the Trust as they may appoint.

d. To furnish the Beneficiary at special meetings, at which the same shall be requested, a careful, accurate, written report of their transactions as Trustees hereunder, of the financial standing of the Trust, and of such other information concerning the affairs of the Trust as they shall request.

e. To sell the Trust Property and distribute the proceeds therefrom:

(1) If any property shall remain in trust under this Agreement for a term which exceeds that allowed under applicable state law, the Trustee forthwith shall sell same at public sale after a reasonable public advertisement and reasonable notice to the Beneficiary and, after deducting its reasonable fees and expenses, the Trustee shall divide the proceeds of the sale among the then Beneficiaries as their interests may then appear, without any direction or consent whatsoever, or

4

(2) To transfer, set over, convey and deliver to all the then Beneficiaries of this Trust their respective undivided interests in any nondivisible assets, or

(3) To transfer, set over and deliver all of the assets of the Trust to its then Beneficiaries, in their respective proportionate shares, at any time when the assets of the Trust consist solely of cash.

7. **Compensation of Trustee**. The Beneficiary jointly and severally agree that the Trustee shall receive reasonable compensation monthly for his services as Trustee hereunder.

8. **Liability of Trustee**. The Trustee and his successor as Trustee shall not be required to give a bond, and each Trustee shall be liable only for his own acts and then only as a result of his own gross negligence or bad faith.

9. **Removal of Trustee**. The Beneficiary shall have the power to remove a Trustee from his office or appoint a successor to succeed him.

10. **Resignation and Successor**.

   a. Any Trustee may resign his office with thirty (30) days written notice to Beneficiary and Beneficiary shall proceed to elect a new Trustee to take the place of the Trustee who had resigned, but the resignation shall not take effect until a certificate thereof, signed, sealed, and acknowledged by the Trustee and a certificate of the election of the new Trustee, signed and sworn to by the Beneficiary and containing an acceptance of the office, signed and acknowledged by the new Trustee, shall have been procured in a form which is acceptable for recording in the registries of deeds of all the counties in which properties held under this instrument are situated. If the Beneficiary shall fail to elect a new Trustee within thirty (30) days after the resignation, then the Trustee may petition any appropriate court in this state to accept his resignation and appoint a new Trustee.

   b. Any vacancy in the office of Trustee, whether arising from death or from any other cause not herein provided for, shall be filled within thirty (30) days from the date of the vacancy and the Beneficiary shall proceed to elect a new Trustee to fill the vacancy, and immediately thereafter shall cause to be prepared a certificate of the election containing an acceptance of the office, signed, sealed, and acknowledged by the new Trustee, which shall be in a form acceptable for recording in the registries of deeds of all the counties in which properties held under this instrument are situated.

c. Whenever a new Trustee shall have been elected or appointed to the office of Trustee and shall have assumed the duties of office, he shall succeed to the title of all the properties of the Trust and shall have all the powers and be subject to all the restrictions granted to or imposed upon the Trustee by this agreement, and every Trustee shall have the powers, rights, and interests regarding the Trust Property, and shall be subject to the same restrictions and duties as the original Trustee, except as the same shall have been modified by amendment, as herein provided for.

d. Notwithstanding any such resignation, the Trustee shall continue to have a lien on the Trust Property for all costs, expenses and attorney's fees incurred and for said Trustee's reasonable compensation.

11. **Objects and Purposes of Trust**. The objects and purposes of this Trust shall be to hold title to the Trust Property and to protect and conserve it until its sale or other disposition or liquidation. The Trustee shall not undertake any activity not strictly necessary to the attainment of the foregoing objects and purposes, nor shall The Trustee transact business within the meaning of applicable state law, or any other law, nor shall this Agreement be deemed to be, or create or evidence the existence of a corporation, de facto or de jure, or a Massachusetts Trust, or any other type of business trust, or an association in the nature of a corporation, or a partnership or joint venture by or between the Trustee and the Beneficiary, or by or between the Beneficiary.

12. **Exculpation**. The Trustee shall have no power to bind the Beneficiary personally and, in every written contract he may enter into, reference shall be made to this declaration; and any person or corporation contracting with the Trustee, as well as any beneficiary, shall look to the funds and the Trust Property for payment under such contract, or for the payment of any debt, mortgage, judgment, or decree, or for any money that may otherwise become due or payable, whether by reason or failure of the Trustee to perform the contract, or for any other reason, and neither the Trustee nor the Beneficiary shall be liable personally therefor.

13. **Dealings with Trustee**. No party dealing with the Trustee in relation to the Trust Property in any manner whatsoever, and,

6

without limiting the foregoing, no party to whom the property or any part of it or any interest in it shall be conveyed, contracted to be sold, leased or mortgaged by the Trustee, shall be obliged to see to the application of any purchase money, rent or money borrowed or otherwise advanced on the property; to see that the terms of this Trust Agreement have been complied with; to inquire into the authority, necessity or expediency of any act of the Trustee, or be privileged to inquire into any of the terms of this Trust Agreement. Every deed, mortgage, lease or other instrument executed by the Trustee in relation to the Trust Property shall be conclusive evidence in favor of every person claiming any right, title or interest under the Trust that at the time of its delivery the Trust created under this Agreement was in full force and effect; and that instrument was executed in accordance with the terms and conditions of this agreement and all its amendments, if any, and is binding upon all Beneficiary under it; that the Trustee was duly authorized and empowered to execute and deliver every such instrument; if a conveyance has been made to a successor or successors in trust, that the successor or successors have been appointed properly and are vested fully with all the title, estate, rights, powers, duties and obligations of its, his or their predecessor in Trust.

14. **Recording of Agreement**. This Agreement shall not be placed on record in the county in which the Trust Property is situated, or elsewhere, but if it is so recorded, that recording shall not be considered as notice of the rights of any person under this Agreement derogatory to the title of powers of the Trustee.

15. **Name of Trustee**. The name of the Trust shall not be used by the Beneficiary in connection with any advertising or other publicity whatever without the written consent of the Trustee.

16. **Income Tax Returns**. The Trustee shall be obligated to file any income tax returns with respect to the Trust, as required by law, and the Beneficiary individually shall report and pay their share of income taxes on the earnings and avails of the Trust Property or growing out of their interest under this Trust.

17. **Assignment**. The interest of a Beneficiary, of any part of that interest, may be transferred only by a written assignment, executed in duplicate and delivered to the Trustee. The Trustee shall note his acceptance on the original and duplicate original of the assignment, retaining the original and delivering the duplicate original to the assignee as and for his of her evidence of ownership of a beneficial interest under this Agreement. No assignment of any interest under this Agreement, other than by operation of law, that is not so executed, delivered and accepted shall be valid without the written approval of all of the other Beneficiaries, if any, who possess the power of direction. No person who is vested with the power of direction, but who is not

7

a Beneficiary under this Agreement, shall assign that power without the written consent of all the Beneficiary.

18. **Individual Liability of Trustee**. The Trustee shall not be required, in dealing with the Trust Property or in otherwise acting under this Agreement, to enter into any individual contract or other individual obligation whatsoever; nor to make himself individually liable to pay or incur the payment of any damages, attorneys' fees, fines, penalties, forfeitures, costs, charges or other sums of money whatsoever. The Trustee shall have no individual liability or obligation whatsoever arising from its ownership, as Trustee, of the legal title to the Trust Property, or with respect to any act done or contract entered into or indebtedness incurred by him in dealing with the Trust Property or in otherwise acting under this Agreement, except only as far as the Trust Property and any trust funds in the actual possession of the Trustee shall be applicable to the payment and discharge of that liability or obligation.

19. **Reimbursement and Indemnification of Trustee**. If the Trustee shall pay or incur any liability to pay any money on account of this Trust, or incur any liability to pay any money on account of being made a party to any litigation as a result of holding title to the Trust Property or otherwise in connection with this Trust, whether because of breach of contract, injury to person or property, fines or penalties under any law, or otherwise, the Beneficiaries, jointly and severally agree that on demand they will pay to the Trustee, with interest at the maximum rate allowed under the laws of the State of Tennessee per annum, all such payments made or liabilities incurred by the Trustee, together with its expenses, including reasonable attorneys' fees, and that they will indemnity and hold the Trustee harmless of and from any and all payments made or liabilities incurred by him for any reason whatsoever as a result of this Agreement; and all amounts so paid by the Trustee, as well as his compensation under this Agreement, shall constitute a lien on the Trust Property. The Trustee shall not be required to convey or otherwise deal with Trust Property as long as any money is due to the Trustee under this Agreement; nor shall the Trustee be required to advance or pay out any money on account of this Trust or to prosecute or defend any legal proceedings involving this Trust or any property or interest under this Agreement unless he shall be furnished with sufficient funds or be indemnified to his satisfaction.

20. **Entire Agreement**. This Agreement contains the entire understanding between the parties and may be amended, revoked, or terminated only by written agreement signed by the Trustee and all of the Beneficiary.

21. **Governing Law**. This Agreement, and all transactions contemplated hereby, shall be governed by, construed and enforced in accordance with the laws of the State of Tennessee applicable to

8

contracts executed and performed in Tennessee. The parties waive any right to a trial by jury and agree to submit to the personal jurisdiction and venue of a court of subject matter jurisdiction located in Davidson County, State of Tennessee. In the event that litigation results from or arises out of this Agreement or the performance thereof, the parties agree to reimburse the prevailing party's reasonable attorney's fees, court costs, and all other expenses, whether or not taxable by the court as costs, in addition to any other relief to which the prevailing party may be entitled. In such event, no action shall be entertained by said court or any court of competent jurisdiction if filed more than one year subsequent to the date the cause(s) of action actually accrued regardless of whether damages were otherwise, as of said time, calculable.

22. **Binding Effect**. The terms and conditions of this Agreement shall inure to the benefit of and be binding upon any successor trustee under it, as well as upon the executors, administrators, heirs, assigns and all other successors-in-interest of the Beneficiary.

23. **Trustee's Liability to Beneficiaries**. The Trustee shall be liable to the Beneficiaries for the value of their respective beneficial interests only to the extent of the property held in Trust by him hereunder and the Beneficiaries shall enforce such liability only against the Trust Property and not against the Trustee personally.

24. **Annual Statements**. There shall be no annual meeting of the Beneficiaries, but the Trustee shall prepare an annual report of their receipts and disbursements for the preceding fiscal year, which fiscal year shall coincide with the calendar year, and a copy of the report shall be sent by mail to the Beneficiaries not later than February 28 of each year.

25. **Termination**. This trust may be terminated at any time by a majority of the Beneficiaries and with thirty (30) days written notice of termination delivered to the Trustee, the Trustee shall execute any and all documents necessary to vest fee simple marketable title to any and all Trust Property in the Beneficiary.

IN WITNESS WHEREOF, the parties hereto have executed this agreement as of the day and year first above written.

Beneficiary:

_____
Robert D. Shemin

_____

STATE OF TENNESSEE
COUNTY OF DAVIDSON

    Personally appeared before me, _____, a Notary Public in and for the State and County aforesaid, **Robert D. Shemin**, the within named bargainor, with whom I am personally acquainted (or proved to me on the basis of satisfactory evidence), and who acknowledged that he executed the foregoing instrument for the purposes therein contained.

    WITNESS my hand and seal at office, on this _____ day of October, 1993.

                                             _____
                                             Notary Public

My Commission Expires:

_____

STATE OF TENNESSEE
COUNTY OF _____

    Personally appeared before me, _____, a Notary Public in and for the State and County aforesaid, _____, the within named bargainor, with whom I am personally acquainted (or proved to me on the basis of satisfactory evidence), and who acknowledged that he executed the foregoing instrument for the purposes therein contained.

    WITNESS my hand and seal at office, on this _____ day of October, 1993.

                                             _____
                                             Notary Public

My Commission Expires:

_____

11

EXHIBIT A

LEGAL DESCRIPTION

EXHIBIT B

BENEFICIARIES AND THEIR INTERESTS

Name and Address	Interest
Robert D. Shemin _____ _____	100%

DESCRIPTION OF OTHER REAL ESTATE OWNED

(ALL DUPLEXES)

Honest Profits

PROPERTY 1

4656-58 FORREST RIDGE DRIVE
HERMITAGE, TENNESSEE

GROSS RENT	$730.00
MINUS PAYMENT	372.00
MINUS TAXES AND INSURANCE	————
FREE CASH FLOW	$358.00/MONTH
TOTAL INVESTMENT	$10,917.00

Appendix

PROPERTY 2

2716 C-D EASTLAND

GROSS RENT	$830.00
MINUS PAYMENT	
MINUS TAXES AND INSURANCE	<u>493.00</u>
FREE CASH FLOW	$337.00/MONTH
TOTAL INVESTMENT	$10,936.00

REHAB WORK SHEET

1. **Cash Out of Pocket:**

    Down Payment _____
    Closing Costs _____
    Appraisal _____
    Termite letter _____
    Survey _____
    Title Ins. _____
    Misc. _____
    Total _____

2. **Cost of Rehab:**

    Flooring _____
    Painting _____
    Roofing _____
    Windows/Screens _____
    Kitchen (faucets, cabinets, etc.) _____
    Bathroom (vanity, sink, tub, etc.) _____
    Bedrooms _____
    Decorations (ceiling fans, brass, etc.) _____
    Doors _____
    Foundation _____
    Fireplace _____
    Locks _____
    Plumbing _____
    Insulation _____
    Total _____

    Total multiplied by a 15% repair cost overrun _____

3. **Estitmated Holding Costs:**

    # Months x
    Mtge._____ + Ins._____ + Taxes_____ + Util._____   _____

4. **Estimated Selling Costs (following rehab)**

    Closing Costs _____
    Attorneys fees _____
    Document/Transfer taxes _____
    Commissions _____
    Total _____

5. **TOTAL EST. ACQUISITION, REHAB & SELLING COSTS** _____
    (Add totals from lines 1, 2, 3 and 4)
    5a.   Plus (+) Mortgage Balance Payoff   +_____

6. **TOTAL COST OF PROPERTY** (Add lines 5 and 5a) _____

7. **TOTAL PROJECTED SELLING PRICE** (following rehab) _____

8. **TOTAL PROFIT** (Subtract Line 6 from Line 7) _____

Appendix

PROPERTY INFORMATION WORKSHEET

Property Address   Referred by:
City   State   Zip

Map/Parcel   Legal   Trust Deed Book/Page_____   Deed Book/Page_____
Current Owner: Phone   Spouse
Date Purchased_____
Purchase Price_____
Mortgage Amount   Interest Rate   %
Years Amortized   P&I   Last Payment Made   Approximate Balance
\# of Elapsed Payments
Amount Needed to Re-instate_____   Pay-Off Amount_____
Mortgage Co.   Contact   Phone
Foreclosure Date   Trustee   Phone
2nd Mortgage Held By
Contact   Phone
Amount   Int. Rate   %   Date Originated   Book Page
Approximate Balance   Account #   Trustee   Ph.#
3rd Mortgage Held By
Contact   Phone
Amount   Int. Rate   %   Date Originated   Book Page
Approximate Balance   Account #   Trustee   Ph.#
Lien: Amount $ Date   Book/Page   Metro Liens: Amount $
Date   Book/Page
IRS Liens:
Amount $ Date   Book/Page   Contact
    Phone

State Tax Liens:
Amount $ Date   Book/Page   Contact   Phone

Bankruptcy: Chapter   Date Filed   Case#   SS#   Attorney
                            Phone   Date Discharged/Dismissed
Relief From Automatic Stay Granted
Neighbor Phone   Neighbor Phone
Other Family Member(s) Phone

NOTES:

PROPERTY ACQUISITION WORKSHEET

ADDRESS:

1. Estimated Sales Price After Fix-Up: $
2. Down Payment
3. Purchase Closing Costs
4. Commission
5. Appraisal
6. Termite
7. Survey
8. Miscellaneous
9. Total Acquisition Expense
10. Repair Budget
11. Cost Overruns
12. Total Fix-Up Costs
13. Payments For _____ Months
14. Property Tax
15. Insurance
16. Utilities
17. Total Holding Costs
18. Sale Closing Costs
19. Commission
20. Advertising, telemarketing
21. Total Sales Costs (Sales Price Less Lines 9, 12, 17, 21)
22. $ Mortgage Pay-Offs

ESTIMATED NET PROFIT:
CASH REQUIREMENT (lines 9, 12, 13, 15, 16, 20):

Appendix

RENTAL UNIT PREPARATION (for office use)

Inspector's initials:

NEW LOCKS

PAINTING

WINDOWS PATCHED

CARPETS CLEANED

APPLIANCES OPERATING/CLEANED

ELECTRICAL OUTLETS/FIXTURES

WATER PIPES/ TOILETS CHECKED FOR LEAKS

YARDS CUT AND DEBRIS PICKED UP

PEST CONTROL SPRAYED

STAIRS, HANDRAILS, PORCHES REPAIRED

SMOKE ALARM TESTED

NICE CLEAN SMELL PRESENT

DRAPES OR BLINDS HUNG AT WINDOWS

ANY SPECIAL ADDED TOUCH

WELCOME CARD LEFT FOR NEW TENANT

Date of Inspection:

MANAGEMENT MOVE-IN CHECKLIST

ADDRESS:

TENANT'S NAME:

DATE:

Application filled out and fee collected:
Verification filed out and fee collected:
Deposit given to reserve rental:
First month's rent collected:
Security deposit collected:
Move-in payment schedule:
Rental Agreement signed and explained:
Additional agreements:
Information sheet for new tenants:
On-time payments emphasized/collection procedures:
Rental inventory sheet given and checked:
Office hours/maintenance:
Request/repair policies explained:
Periodic inspections discussed:
Renter's insurance suggested:

VACANCY MAKE-OVER CHECKLIST

1. Check and test all wall receptacles and switches. One faulty switch affect the overall safety of the electrical system.
2. Turn on/off all faucets. Check for leaks, also around the tub, shower-heads and under sink.
3. Flush toilets. Make sure they are functioning properly, no leaks around bottom, maintains water, and shuts off properly.
4. Close and open all doors, exterior, interior, sliding and closets. Check door stops.
5. If drapes are provided, clean or order replacements.
6. Clean and vacuum all carpets.
7. Exterminate for all pests.
8. Replace light bulbs if out. Good lighting helps show vacant units.
9. Clean (in, behind and under) and check all appliances. Make sure all appliances are running effectively.
10. Make sure all countertops, drawers, and cabinets are clean. Remove old shelf paper. Check to see that all hardware is in place.
11. Make bathrooms shine (tubs, sink, mirrors, all tile, medicine cabinets and vanities). Remove any decals, etc. Paint if necessary.
12. Make sure all bathroom details are in place(towel-bars, toilet paper holders, soap dishes).
13. Check condition of paint on all interior walls/ceilings. Paint if necessary. Fill in any holes.
14. Clean and shine all vinyl flooring.
15. Clean all windows and mirrors. Replace any broken or scratched windows. Check to see if all screens are in place and whether they are torn.
16. Check heating units and air conditioners, including replacing filters.
17. Remove all debris or personal items left.
18. Put air freshener in place.
19. Sweep entryways and wash off front of building/house. Does front porch need painting?
20. Re-key all locks and ensure all are working properly. See if any window locks are needed.
21. Is exterior of premises clean and neat? Does grass need cutting or other landscaping needs?

Checklist Complete: Date:

Honest Profits

RENTAL APPLICATION

Applicant wants to lease——————————————————————————————

Applicant wants to move in—————————————————————————————

Application Fee——————————————————

Date of Application——————————— Applicant's Name——————————————

Social Security # ————————————— Children's Names & Ages————————————

Present Address————————————————————————— How Long?——————

Present Landlord's Name————————————————————— Phone #———————

Previous Address——————————————————————————— How Long?——————

Previous Landlord's Name—————————————————————— Phone #———————

Have you ever paid the rent late?————— Why?————————————————————

Employer——————————————————— Employer's Address————————————

Supervisor——————————————————— Your Job Title———————————————

Length of Service——————————————— Salary per Week———————————————

Supervisor's Phone #———————————————————— Any arrest record?——————

Credit References with Phone #'s:
1.——
2.——
3.——

Car Financed?————— Name of Company——————————— Address————————

Furniture Financed?——— Name of Company——————————— Address————————

Applicant's Driver's License #————————————————————— State——————

MDHA Case Worker——————————————————————————————————

In Case of an Emergency:
Name————————————— Address——————————— Phone #——————

Relation————————————— Doctor's Name——————————————————
I hereby authorize   to submit the information I have given for verification
and I specifically authorize   to contact the employers, landlords, banks,
Police for any police records, and other credit references which I have listed above for
the purpose of verifying the information furnished by me in this application.

———————————————————
Applicant's Signature

Appendix

LOAN QUALIFICATION WORKSHEET

The following worksheet will allow you to calculate the mortgage loan amount for which you qualify.

MAXIMUM DEBT ALLOWED

Stable Monthly Income $ _____
(Multiply by .28)   x 28%
Maximum Monthly Housing Expense   = $ _____
Stable Monthly Income $ _____
(Multiply by .36)   x 36%
Maximum Monthly Housing Expense
Plus Other Obligations   = $ _____

ACTUAL AND ANTICIPATED EXPENSES

Monthly Housing Expense		Total Monthly Expenses	
Principal + Interest	$ _____	Total Housing	$ _____
Real Estate Taxes	$ _____	Installment Debt	$ _____
Insurance Premium	$ _____	Revolving Charges	$ _____
Homeowner Assoc.	$ _____	Alimony, Etc.	$ _____
		Other	$ _____
Total	$ _____	Total	$ _____

Compare actual to maximum expenses allowed. Actual expenses should not exceed the maximum allowed.

These qualifications are the standard current guidelines used by most lenders in your area.

Honest Profits

Personal Financial Statemer

To: _____ (the Bank) Office _____

Please read the following directions before completing this Personal Financial Statement.

1. Complete all sections, except Section 2, if you are applying for individual credit in your own name and are relying solely on your ow income or assets for repayment or if this personal financial statement relates to your guaranty of the indebtedness of other person(s firm(s), or corporation(s).

2. Also, complete Section 2 if any of the following apply:

   - If you are applying for joint credit with another person, provide information about the joint applicant.

   - If you are relying on income from alimony, child support, or separate maintenance or on the income or assets of another person as basis for repayment of the credit requested, provide information about the person on whose alimony, support or maintenanc payments or income or assets you are relying.

   - If this is a joint guaranty of the indebtedness of other person(s), firm(s), corporation(s), provide information about the joint guarantor.

Section 1 - Individual/Applicant Information (Please Print)	Section 2 - Other Party/Co-Applicant Information
Name	Name
Residence Address	Residence Address
City / State / Zip Code	City / State / Zip Code
Position or Occupation	Position or Occupation
Business Name	Business Name
Business Address	Business Address
City / State / Zip Code	City / State / Zip Code
Years with Business	Years with Business
Res. Phone ( ) / Bus. Phone ( )	Res. Phone ( ) / Bus. Phone ( )

Appendix

Statement of Financial Condition as of _____, 19 ____

Section 3 - Balance Sheet (attach additional schedules as needed)

Assets	Dollars	Jt°	Liabilities	Dollars	Jt°
Cash and Short-term Investments (Schedule A)			Outstanding Credit Card Balances		
Stocks & Bonds (readily marketable) (Schedule B)			Taxes Payable		
Unlisted Securities (Schedule C)			Policy Loan (life insurance) (Schedule D)		
Notes Receivable & Accounts Receivable			Mortgages & Obligations Due (Schedules F & G)		
Cash Surrender Value-Life Insurance (Schedule D)			Notes & Accounts Payable (Schedule H)		
General/Ltd Partnership Interests (Schedule E)			Other Liabilities (list):		
Retirement Accounts					
Personal Property					
Automobiles					
Real Estate-Personal Residences (Schedule F)					
Real Estate-Investments (Schedule G)					
Real Estate Investments (Direct & Partnership Interests) (Schedule I)**					
Other Assets (list):					
TOTAL ASSETS			**TOTAL LIABILITIES**		
			NET WORTH (total assets minus total liabilities)		

Section 4 - Income Statement

Annual Income	Applicant	Co-Applicant	Annual Expenses	Applicant	Co-Applicant
Salary			Home Mortgage (Principal & Interest)		
Bonus and Commissions			Loan Payments (including other R/E)		
Interest and Dividends			Income Tax (State & Federal)		
Alimony, Separate Maintenance, Child Support***			Planned or Required Investments/ Partnership Contributions		
Capital Gains			General Living Expenses		
Real Estate Income			Other Expenses (list):		
Other Income (list):					
GROSS INCOME $	$		**TOTAL EXPENSES** $	$	

Section 5 - Contingent Liabilities (include brief description)

	Applicant	Co-Applicant
As endorser or guarantor on notes/leases/contracts:		
On letters of credit:		
Current or pending suits or other litigation:		
Other (Partnership, etc.) explain:		
TOTAL $	$	

°Please check if jointly held.

**Schedule I should be used by individuals with extensive real estate investments where additional data may be needed or required by the Bank to properly evaluate the borrower's financial condition. It can be used instead of Schedule G. Because it will not be completed by most borrowers or guarantors, it is a separate schedule not printed on this Personal Financial Statement. If it is appropriate for you and has not been provided, please request it from the Bank.

***Alimony, separate maintenance, and/or child support income need not be revealed if you do not wish to have it considered as a basis for repaying this obligation.

Honest Profits

Schedule A: Cash & Short-term Investments (certificates of deposit, commercial paper, money market funds, etc.)

Name of Institution	Savings Accts ($ amount)	Checking Accts ($ amount)	Other Short-term Investments (type and $ amount)	Total	Pledged? (Y)/(N)	Owner(s) Code*

Schedule B: Stocks and Bonds (include U.S. Government and Marketable Securities)

Number of Shares or Face Value (Bonds)	Description	Market Value	Margin? (Y)/(N)	Restricted? (Y)/(N)	Pledged? (Y)/(N)	Owner(s) Code*

Schedule C: Unlisted Securities

Number of Shares	Description	Source of Value	Value	% of Company Owned	Pledged? (Y)/(N)	Owner(s) Code*

Schedule D: Life Insurance Carried (include individual and group insurance)

Name of Insurance Company	Owner of Policy	Beneficiary	Face Value	Policy Loans	Cash Surrender Value	Assigned? (Y)/(N)

Schedule E: General and/or Limited Partnership Interests (Please attach K-1)

Name of Partnership	Type of Investment	(L)imited (G)eneral	Amount Invested	Fair Market Value of Interest	Annual Contribution Required	Pledged? (Y)/(N)	Owner(s) Code*

*Owner(s) Code: A=Applicant   AC=Joint Account of Applicant and Co-Applicant   JC=Joint Account of Co-Applicant and another party
               C=Co-Applicant   JA=Joint Account of Applicant and another party

Appendix

Schedule F: Real Estate (Personal Residences)

Description/Address of Property	Mortgage Holder	Maturity Date	Title in Name of	Purchase Date	Cost	Present Loan Balance	Monthly Payt.	Market Value

Schedule G: Real Estate Investments

Description/Address of Property	Mortgage Holder	Maturity Date	% Owned	Title in Name of	Purchase Date	Cost	Present Loan Balance	Market Value	Total Annual Rental Income	Monthly Loan Payt.	Other Expenses

Schedule H: Notes & Accounts Payable (also include credit lines and other commitments even if unused)

Name of Creditor	Orig. Amt. of Loan	Payment/Repayment Terms	Maturity Date	Interest Rate	Description of Collateral (if any)	Balance Owing	Debtor(s) Code*

*Debtor(s) Code: A—Applicant AC—Joint Account of Applicant and Co-Applicant JC—Joint Account of Co-Applicant and another party
C—Co-Applicant JA—Joint Account of Applicant and another party

Personal Information

Do you have a will? ☐ Yes ☐ No If yes, name of executor:
Dependents Number: Ages:

Are you a partner or officer in any venture other than described on schedules? ☐ Yes ☐ No If yes, describe:

Are any assets pledged other than as described on schedules? ☐ Yes ☐ No If yes, describe:

Have you ever been declared bankrupt? ☐ Yes ☐ No If yes, describe:

Are there any outstanding judgements against you? ☐ Yes ☐ No
Do you have disability insurance? ☐ Yes ☐ No
Income tax settled through (date)
Alimony, Child Support/Maintenance Expense $

The information contained in this statement is provided for the purpose of obtaining, or maintaining credit with the Bank on behalf of the undersigned or person, firms or corporations in whose behalf the undersigned may either severally or jointly with others, execute a guaranty in the Bank's favor. Each undersigned understands that the Bank is relying on the information provided herein (including the designation made as to ownership of property) in deciding to grant or continue credit. Each undersigned represents and warrants that the information provided is true and complete and that the Bank may consider this statement as continuing to be true and correct until a written notice of a change is given to the Bank by the undersigned. The Bank is authorized to make all inquiries it deems necessary to verify the accuracy of the statements made herein, and to determine the credit worthiness of the undersigned. The Bank is authorized to answer questions about its credit experience with the undersigned.

Date Signed	Signature (individual)	Social Security #	Date of Birth
Date Signed	Signature (other party)	Social Security #	Date of Birth

Loan Request

1804 Fatherland Street -- 4 bedroom, 1 1/2 bath, Historic Edgefield

This is a completely rennovated historic home in Edgefield. It has hardwood floors, large rooms, a deck, high ceilings. Everything in the house has been completely redone. Next door, on one side, lives the assistant symphony conductor who paid over $100,000 for her home. On the other side is a 2 bedroom house that is listed for $82,000. I have a contract on the house to lease/purchase it for $78,000; $800/ month rent.

    Appraisal Value = $75,000- $85,000
    Gross Rent = $800/ month
    Vacancy and Repairs = $50/ month
        Lease/ Purchase
    Taxes and Insurance = $69/ month
    Net Rent = $681/ month

1st Mortgage Payment = $507/ month
    ($50,000 loan, 9%, 180 months)

Property has no debt on it.

Greenwood Court Project

Brief Description

Sixteen brick duplexes each containing two 2-bedroom, 1-bath apartments of about 850 square feet, located in a nice area of East Nashville. All but about 8 units are rented for between $355.00 - $400.00 a month. Over 90% of the tenants are on the Section 8 program which means the government pays all or most of the rent. All of the tenants and rents qualify as low or very low income according to the Department of Housing and Urban Development.

The vacancies are due to the fact that they are the last ones to be rehabilitated. All of the other units have just gone through a major rehabilitation. The units are located in a dead end court which enable the owner to control the area.

Long Term Plan

To rent the majority of the units to Section 8 tenants. Some of the units may be converted to 3 bedrooms to increase the rents to about $450.00 a side as opposed to $375.00 a side. The cost to do this is about $1,000.00 a unit. Though demand for 2 bedroom units is high, the demand for 3 bedroom units is incredibly high.

The Section 8 Program

This program is for low income families mainly led by single mothers with children. The money is allotted for 10 years for each certificate holder or tenant, by HUD and administered by M.D.H.A.

The leases are guaranteed for a year. Usually, the government pays all of the rent. Sometimes the tenant has to pay a small amount. M.D.H.A. inspects the units twice a year and requires them to be in good repair.

Section 8 and M.D.H.A. also insure against damages for up to 2 months rent, about $750.00 for each unit. If the tenant damages the unit, the landlord can collect the damage money from Section 8.

The demand for Section 8 housing is extremely high. The quantity and quality of housing available for Section 8 tenants is very low. Thus, I have been operating my 20 duplexes at a 100% occupancy rate with waiting lists for each property. The landlord can screen the tenants, and does not have to rent to someone he or she does not want to rent to.

Financial Details

Per building purchase price	$39,000.00
18% down payment	7,020.00
Amount financed	31,980.00
Monthly payment, 15 years @ 8.5 interest	314.92
Taxes per month	40.00
Insurance per month	25.00
Monthly payment w/taxes and insurance	379.92
Current rent per duplex	750.00
<u>Free cash flow per month.</u>	<u>370.08</u>

Risks

Vacancy and repair risks are inherent in real estate. The vacancy risk should be about 0. Again, the demand for Section 8 housing is high. I have not advertised in almost a year and have kept my 20 duplexes full. I get about 10 - 20 calls a week from people looking for housing. Furthermore, the Greenwood project is in an excellent location. The repair cost is also minimal because Section 8 guarantees about 2 month's rent for damage repair. That is about $750.00 per unit. All of my appliances are insured, so it is very difficult for a tenant to do more than $750.00 worth of damage, especially if they are managed properly. Also, only one side of each duplex has to stay rented in order to pay the note, taxes and insurance.

Management

I personally manage all of my properties. I walk through each unit at least once every 30 days. I have and intend to provide the highest quality low and moderate income housing in Davidson County. All of my units are like new when the tenants move in, and I try to keep them that way.

I use licensed, bonded contractors for all of my repairs. They work for about $7.00 an hour and do quality work. Thus, whatever repairs I do incur are handled promptly, professionally and reasonably.

Appendix

REAL ESTATE SCHEDULE FOR ROBERT SHEMIN
DATE: 10-01-92

DUPLEXES

	1 4656-4658 FOREST RIDGE	2 4625-4627 FOREST RIDGE	3 4653-4655 FOREST RIDGE	4 2300-2302 CAMPBELL
TITLE	Robert Shemin	Robert Shemin	Robert Shemin	Robert Shemin
PURCHASE PRICE	$39,000	$38,700	$48,000	$47,500
YEAR PURCHASED	1991	1991	1991	1991
APPRAISED VALUE	$50,000	$49,000	$53,000	$54,000
DEBT	$34,000	$33,900	$38,450	$39,000
MORTGAGE HOLDER	Kislak	Kislak	Kislak	Kislak
MONTHLY PAYMENT TAXES AND INSURANCE INCLUDED	428.00	404.00	450.00	422.00
GROSS MONTHLY RENT	740.00	739.00	730.00	750.00
GROSS MONTHLY INCOME	$312	$335	$280	$328
TOTAL FREE CASH FLOW		$6,767		
VACANCY & REPAIRS EXPENSE		$1,200		
90% of leases are Section 8 which are guranteed for a year.				
MONTHLY INCOME		$5,567		
TOTAL EQUITY		$362,862		

165

OPTION TO PURCHASE REAL ESTATE

This agreement, made this _____ day of _____, 19___, by and between _____ hereinafter called Optionor, and _____ hereinafter called Optionee, Witnesseth, that for and in consideration of the sum of:

_____ Dollars ($) paid by Optionee to Optionor, the receipt whereof is hereby acknowledged, the Optionor hereby give and grant unto the Optionee heirs, personal representatives, and assigns, the right of purchasing, on or before the _____ day of _____, 19____, the following described real estate situated in _____ County, State, to-wit:

_____

for the total purchase price of _____ Dollars ($).
Shall be paid as follows _____
If the Optionee elect(s) to purchase the said real estate pursuant to this Option, Optionee shall give notice to such Optionor, at _____. on or before the ____ day of _____, 19__.

    If the Optionee shall so elect to purchase said real estate, and shall give of such election as herein provided within the time required, and shall tender the required amount of cash, and a real estate contract or other security to Optionor, on the real estate hereinabove particularly described, then Optionor agree to convey the real estate to Optionee heirs, and assigns, by warranty deed, free and clear of all liens, encumbrances, or taxes to the date of closing of the purchase. Optionor further agree, that upon such election by Optionee, to deliver to Optionee, within 30 days after receipt of such written notice of election to purchase, a policy of title insurance in the full sum of the purchase price showing merchantable title to said real estate.

    If the Optionee do not exercise the privilege of purchase given and do not fully perform the conditions herein within the time herein stated, the privilege shall wholly cease and terminate and the sum of _____ Dollars($), herein paid by Optionee shall be retained by Optionor.

    The right by either party to terminate this agreement for failure to perform or observe the obligations, agreements or covenants of this agreement, the party at fault shall pay all reasonable attorney's fees and expenses of the other party.

    This agreement constitutes the entire agreement of the parties hereto and may not be modified except by a written document signed by all parties.

    IN WITNESS WHEREOF, the parties have executed this the day and year first above written.

_____   _____
Optionor   Optionee

CONTRACT OF SALE

THIS CONTRACT of sale made this _____, 19_____, by and between _____ hereinafter called the seller, and _____ hereinafter called the buyer;

WITNESSETH: That the seller in considerations of the sum of _____ DOLLARS as earnest money and in part payment of the purchase price has this day sold and does hereby agree to convey by a good and valid warranty deed to said buyer, or to such person as he may in writing direct, the following described real estate in _____ county, Tennessee, to-wit:

CONSIDERATION: Buyer agrees to purchase said real estate and to pay therefor the sum of _____ DOLLARS, upon the following terms:
$_____ cash, balance

MISCELLANEOUS CONDITIONS:

TITLE INSURANCE: The _____ or his agent, at seller's expense, agrees to make application to the _____ for Title Insurance on the above property and if, after examination by this Company the title is found insurable the buyer hereby agrees to accept a Title Policy issued by said Company in it's usual form and to comply with this contract WITHIN TEN DAYS after receiving a report on the title, and it is agreed that such report shall be conclusive evidence of good title subject to the exceptions therein stated, otherwise that the earnest money is to be refunded.

Should the buyer default in the performance of this contract on his part at the time and in the manner specified then at seller's option the earnest money shall be forfeited as liquidated damages. But such forfeiture shall not prevent suit for the specific performance of this contract.

In the event of default in the terms of this contract for any reason on the part of the seller and in the event it becomes necessary, due to any fault of the seller, that the earnest money herein above shown, must be returned to the buyer, then the seller shall be liable to the agent herein for the full commission set out in this contract.

The words "seller" and "buyer" when used in this contract shall be construed as plural whenever the number of parties to this contract so requires.

SELLER ACKNOWLEDGEMENT: Seller acknowleges that buyer is a licensed Real Estate Broker and is purchasing said property for rental or resale

ADJUSTMENTS TO BE MADE AT TIME OF CLOSING; -
   (1) Sellers Escrow Deposits to be _____
   (2) Taxes for Current Year _____
   (3) Sellers Fire Insurance to be _____
   (4) Existing Leases or Rents_____
Possession to be given_____
Conveyance to be subject to existing Building Restrictions and/or Zoning Ordinances_____
_____Seller
to bear risk of hazard loss to date of deed

Purchaser_____ Seller_____
Purchaser_____ Seller_____

Deed Property to:_____

Honest Profits

CONTRACTOR/SUBCONTRACTOR
POLICY AND PROCEDURE

There are no exceptions to the following policies and procedures:

- All contracts must be in writing and as detailed as possible.
- No checks will be issued without written contracts and invoices.
- Regarding draws, a maximum of 1/3 (one-third) of the total bid will be given up front to cover materials. The balance will not be paid until all work is complete. Absolutely complete. If one door knob is loose, or one sink has a small leak the balance will not be paid.
- The balance will not be paid until all of the contractors trash is removed.
- Service calls will not be paid until they are completed and verified by the tenant that they are complete.
- Contractor will give a date for the completion of a job. If the job is not complete, then the landlord loses money by not being able to rent out the property. Therefore, a $50.00 per day penalty will be deducted from the contractor's final draw for each day, including weekends, that the job is not done.
- On houses for Section 8, 20% of the total will be held back until the unit passes the Section 8 inspection.
- A $25.00 bonus will be paid for units that pass the Section 8 inspection the first time.
- Contractor will guarantee work for six months.
- Contractor must show proof of Workman's Compensation insurance. If not the premiums will be deducted from the cost of the job and paid by the owner or property manager.
- All contractors must sign and agree to this contractor's agreement and attached agreement regarding liability and contractor's status as a contractor and not an employee.

Owner manager   Contractor

Appendix

ABOUT THE AUTHOR

Robert H. Shemin was born in Memphis, Tennessee in 1963. In 1985, Shemin graduated from Vanderbilt University with a B.A. in History. Following Vanderbilt, Shemin left Tennessee to attend Emory University in Atlanta, Georgia. There, he earned two additional degrees—a Master's in Business Administration (MBA) and a Juris Doctorate (law) degree.

Fluent in Spanish, Shemin then traveled to San Jose, Costa Rica to work for the Inter-American Court of Human Rights—one of the world's international court systems. He served as Chief Clerk to the Chief Judge, briefing judges on international law issues and human rights law. He also delivered seminars on human rights law to government officials.

Back in the states, Shemin was hired by the investment banking house, Goldman Sachs & Co. in New York. There, he was trained in all aspects of securities sales, including equities, fixed income and special investments.

Following his tenure at Goldman Sachs, Shemin became a partner in a boutique financial firm, Southeast Financial Group, in Nashville, Tennessee. There, he performed detailed business planning, and tax, estate and investment analysis for his clients.

It was at Southeast Financial Group that Shemin first discovered his interest in real estate. Shemin spent the next six months looking at all aspects of real estate management before buying his first property. In as little as 4 years, Shemin:

- Completed over 250 real estate deals, purchased over 80 properties and manages more than 135 rental units.

- Personally placed over $500,000 of mortgages in the last two quarters of '94.

- Owns and manages a real estate portfolio worth more than $4.0 million.

- Represented sophisticated investors in more than 50 complex real estate transactions.

- Lectures on how to constantly locate under-valued properties.

- Consults with and represents a number of non-profit organizations, providing quality housing for Bosnian, Vietnamese, Haitian and Kurdish refugees and indigents.

- Helped more than 20 home families move into nice clean homes.

- Bought real estate from numerous government organizations—HUD, RTC, VA.

- Been awarded over $400,000 in housing tax credits.

- Approved as an attorney for real estate closings with two of the largest title companies.

- Became a licensed real estate agent.

Shemin lives with his wife, Patricia, and son, Alexander, in Nashville, Tennessee.

$19.95 VALUE!

DEAR BOOK BUYERS
As a special thanks for buying my book
you can get a Free Special Report:

You Could Lose Your Shirt If You Don't Know...

The 25 Most Costly Mistakes Almost Every Real Estate Investor Makes And How To Avoid them

NAME: _____

STREET ADDRESS: _____

CITY/STATE/ZIP: _____

MAIL TO: Robert Shemin, P.O. Box 128186, Nashville, TN 37212-8186